Twayne's United States Authors Series

Sylvia E. Bowman, *Editor*

INDIANA UNIVERSITY

Henry Timrod

HENRY TIMROD

by EDD WINFIELD PARKS

University of Georgia

 TUSAS 53

Twayne Publishers, Inc.   ::   New York

TO

JAY B. HUBBELL

GOOD FRIEND, AND INTELLIGENT WORKER
IN AMERICAN AND IN SOUTHERN LITERATURE

Preface

IN ONE RESPECT, I have deviated slightly from the normal pattern of Twayne's United States Authors Series. Since there is no good or even reasonably reliable biography of Henry Timrod, I have used more space for this subject than would normally be required, and I have given what may seem a disproportionate amount of documentation. I do not think so. Even with this amount of space, I have not untied all the knotty problems in the Timrod biography, especially in the period (1850-59) when he worked as tutor on various plantations for indeterminate periods. At the same time, it has seemed necessary to remember that this is not primarily a biography, but a critical study of a distinguished, if minor, poet and critic. I have tried to present his positive accomplishments without minimizing his literary defects.

To do this, I have tried not only to give an accurate biographical record, but to relate Timrod's life to those of his literary fellow workers. Charleston in the 1850's was an exciting town intellectually. Although only William Gilmore Simms can with strict justness be called a professional man of letters, the number of gifted amateur writers was amazingly high. Simms, Timrod, William J. Grayson, Paul Hamilton Hayne, S. Henry Dickson, John della Torre, John Dickson Bruns, Basil Gildersleeve, and other men met together frequently; they read their poems and articles to each other; they argued violently yet amicably; they whetted their minds by a stimulating process of intellectual attrition. By common consent, Timrod was looked upon as their best poet, and one of their best critics.

His poetry falls into three major groupings. A confirmed Romantic in the tradition of Wordsworth, he wrote often and effectively on nature, although he could never find in it quite the healing power that Wordsworth had. Timrod was troubled by doubts and uncertainties, and by the strange meanings that seemed to underlie his dreams and subconscious thoughts. He was also aroused to poetic fervor by various young ladies, including the one who became his wife. These poems are deftly written; a few are genuinely moving. Since I believe that Timrod's achievements in these fields have been unduly neglected, I have tried to examine the best of these poems fairly and intensively.

Timrod's finest poems deal with the Civil War. Yet in one respect his reputation has suffered because he has been labeled the "Laureate of the Confederacy." This fairly describes his poems at the beginning of the war. But he turned increasingly from strictly martial poems to works that emphasized the tragedy of war, regardless of who won or lost. In a sense, he became a poet of peace in such poems as "Christmas" and "Spring." It is this reading of his best poems that seems to me the correct one; I hope that I have presented this interpretation effectively.

As critic, Timrod insisted that poetry must have an ethical content and an artistic form. He defended Milton and Wordsworth against the attacks of Poe, and argued for the validity and unity of long poems. Beauty was one legitimate province of poetry, but it was not the sole one: the greatest poetry must effectively combine beauty, truth, and power. Timrod was a traditional critic, and at least two of his essays—"Literature in the South," in which he denies the validity of a narrow regionalism, and "A Theory of Poetry"—seem to me important and readable documents in American intellectual history.

A major difficulty has been that little trustworthy work has been done on Timrod. Shortly after his death, his friends Hayne, Simms, and Bruns wrote perceptively about him and his work, but postwar poverty forced them too often to rely on faulty memories. Later commentators have in turn perpetuated the earlier errors, and frequently have added a few of their own. In recent times, there have been some excellent scholarly and critical articles, which I have included with brief descriptions in the bibliography. But I know of only three books, all specialized, that can be relied on: Jay B. Hubbell, *The Last Years of Henry Timrod* (1941); Guy A. Cardwell, Jr., *The Uncollected Poems of Henry Timrod* (1942); and (immodest as I fear it may seem) my own work, *The Essays of Henry Timrod* (1942). We need a collected edition of his letters, and a carefully edited, sensibly arranged edition, with variant readings, of the poems included in the 1899 Memorial Edition.

There are four major sources of manuscript information. One

Preface

is the Paul Hamilton Hayne Collection in the Duke University Library. Dr. Hubbell has reprinted all of the relevant Timrod-Hayne letters in his book. I am indebted to him for permission to use this material, and to him and to Jay B. Hubbell, Jr., for constant and intelligent help with other material in the Duke Library. A second source is the letters to Rachel Lyons (later Mrs. Heustis), now deposited in the University of Alabama Library; these have been printed by William Fidler in the *Southern Literary Messenger* and in the *Alabama Review;* before the final group appeared, Mr. Fidler sent me photostats of the letters and graciously permitted me to use some of the material before his own work was in print. The third source is the Timrod material in the Charleston Library Society, especially in the William A. Courtenay Collection. Mr. Cardwell and I have made extensive use of the Timrod manuscripts in the past; once again, I was given complete access to them, and freedom to use anything that might contribute to this study. For this I am grateful to the officials of the Charleston Library Society. The fourth source, least used but not least important, is in the South Caroliniana Library at the University of South Carolina. The letters and the papers in the Goodwin Collection have been especially helpful. Mr. E. L. Inabinett, the Director, expertly steered me to other useful sources of information, and gave me permission to use what I needed. I am also personally indebted to Mrs. George Munro Goodwin of Athens, Georgia, for permitting me to examine and to use the Timrod manuscripts in her possession.

As always, the officials of my own library have been unfailingly helpful in securing material; among these, Porter Kellam, John Marshall, John Bonner, Sue Fan Tate, and Christine Burroughs. For relief from teaching and aid in my research, I am indebted to Deans Gerald B. Huff, Robert McRorie, and John O. Eidson; for reading the typescript and for making valuable suggestions, to my colleagues John O. Eidson and Rayburn S. Moore. Most of all, for consistently intelligent and unselfish aid, I am indebted to my wife, Aileen Wells Parks.

E. W. P.

Athens, Georgia
October 15, 1962

Contents

Chronology

1828   Henry Timrod, born in Charleston, South Carolina, December 8.

1836   Before July, was attending the German Friendly Society school.

1840   By this time, was attending the Classical School of Christopher Cotes. Paul Hamilton Hayne and Basil Gildersleeve were among his schoolmates.

1845   Entered University of Georgia in January, as an irregular sophomore.

1846   Left, without taking degree, before beginning of August term. Contributed at least two poems to Charleston *Evening News*, September 8 and 16; signed T. H.

1847–   Read law in office of James L. Petigru; but he never
1849   practiced.

1848–   Studied at home in effort to prepare himself for a uni-
1849   versity professorship in the classics; in January, 1849, began contributing to the *Southern Literary Messenger*, under the pseudonym "Aglaus." Quickly became a fairly regular contributor to this publication.

1850–   Worked as tutor on various plantations, including those
1861   of a Mr. Lowndes, Daniel Blake, Murray Robinson, and Dr. Joseph Hazel; taught in Hugh Train's academy at Bluffton in 1860.

1857–   Contributed regularly both poems and essays (often
1860   anonymously) to *Russell's Magazine*.

1859   Published *Poems* through Ticknor and Fields, Boston; book appeared before December 22, 1859.

1861   Published "Ethnogenesis" as a broadside and in *Living Age*, March 30, 1861. Enlisted temporarily in militia company at Hardeeville, July.

1862   Enlisted as Private in Confederate Army in February; detailed as Private Secretary to Col. L. M. Keitt. On three-month leave of absence, served as war correspondent on western front. Became engaged to Katie Goodwin. Because of ill health, given discharge from army in December. In late autumn, plans made for an English edition of his poems; it never appeared.

1863   Became assistant editor of Charleston *Mercury* in August. Re-enlisted in July, but a severe hemorrhage forced him to resign after one day of service.

1864   Moved to Columbia, January 12, to become Associate Editor of the Columbia *Daily South Carolinian.* Wrote most of the editorials until Columbia was captured and burned, February 17, 1865. Married Katie S. Goodwin on February 16, 1864. Their only child, Willie, was born on Christmas Eve.

1865   Wrote some articles and editorials for the *Daily South Carolinian,* which had moved to Charleston, and for the Columbia *Phoenix;* rarely, if ever, paid. Willie died on October 23.

1866   Worked at various temporary jobs; attempted with his sister Emily to open a school, but it failed to develop. His "Ode" sung at Magnolia Cemetery on June 16.

1867   Worked as assistant private secretary to Governor J. L. Orr; twice visited Hayne at Copse Hill, near Augusta, Georgia. Died on October 7, 1867, after long having suffered from tuberculosis.

1873   Hayne Edition of Timrod's poems published.

1899   Memorial Edition of poems published.

Henry Timrod

Biography

I *Ancestry*

HENRY TIMROD'S GRANDFATHER was born in Kusel, Rheinpfalz, Germany, and emigrated to South Carolina in 1765. At that time his name was anglicized from Heinrich Dimroth to Henry Dimrod, and later to Henry Timrod. He set up shop as a merchant tailor and possibly also as a shoemaker, and prospered; as soon as he had amassed enough money, he bought a plantation at Parker's Ferry on Charleston Neck. Before the Revolution he was president of the German Friendly Society; at the outbreak of the war, the German Fusiliers was organized, with Henry Timrod the first name on its roll. He was elected orderly-sergeant of the company, and took part in the expedition against Port Royal and the siege of Savannah. In 1785 he married for the third time; this wife, the grandmother of the poet, had migrated from Northern Ireland to Philadelphia to Charleston, and the marriage was duly recorded in the official newspaper: "Last Saturday night was married, incognito, Henry Timrod, Taylor, to his amiable Housekeeper, Mrs. Susannah Hagan, lately arrived from the northward." [1]

A son, and the father to be of Henry Timrod, William Henry Timrod, was born July 15, 1792. Two years later his father died. Paul Hamilton Hayne wrote that "the family means, already reduced by the exigencies of a revolutionary time," were further straitened by an unwise second marriage. William's daughter Emily, always jealous for her family, did not object to this statement, but she resented Judge George S. Bryan's statements that her father had received his education at a free school: "My mother is my authority for denying this, as she knows that he was one of the pupils of Dr. Bess who kept then one of the best schools in Charleston. . . . her eldest brother was also one of Dr. Bess' scholars."

At the age of eleven William Henry Timrod was apprenticed to the firm of John and Benjamin Crow, stationers and book-binders, in order to learn bookbinding. Hayne indicates that this was the boy's own choice; he was at school, and his mother planned for him to become a lawyer, but in order "to live thence-forth in a beatified atmosphere of Russia leather, he ran away from school, and having found his Phoenix—a complacent book-binder—placed himself deliberately under his tuition." The job demanded skill in craftsmanship, but no knowledge of what might be on the printed pages. According to his daughter, when the thrifty proprietor refused to furnish a candle at night, "I have heard him declare that he used, when the moon was clear, or at its full, to climb on the leads of the house, and there, by the lunar rays, to read into the small hours of the night. Shakespeare was, at that time, his favorite companion." [2]

He read widely if unsystematically in English literature, and he wrote enough lyric poems to publish, undoubtedly at his own expense, a volume entitled *Poems on Various Subjects* (1814). The subjects are familiar enough, and even then a bit well-worn: poems on the eagle and the mockingbird, on an autumn day in Carolina, and on local events. William Henry Timrod was aware of the new Romantic poets, but his taste had been formed by earlier English poetry; at his best he wrote simply, gracefully, unoriginally of that which he had seen or known. Possibly one poem attained more than a local reputation: Judge George S. Bryan, friend of father and son, wrote to Hayne that "As one proof of the excellence of the ode, 'To Time,' let me say here what it would have delighted me to have said to the author, that on my reciting this poem to Washington Irving, he exclaimed with fervor, that 'Tom Moore had written no finer lyric.'" [3]

With some financial aid from the Parker's Ferry farm, in 1812 William bought the bookbindery at 25 Broad Street. Later that year, on December 19, 1812, he married sixteen-year-old Thyrza Prince. The few contemporary accounts that are extant indicate that she was beautiful and good-natured; perhaps with some prejudice, her daughter Emily wrote to Hayne that "The perfec-tion of her face and form caught the poet's *fancy;* the perfection of her character won and kept his HEART through the twenty-six years of their married life." Her parents were Charles Prince, of English descent, and a pioneer Methodist in South Carolina, and Sarah Faesch, daughter of an artillery officer in the Continental Army and of Hannah Caesar.[4]

William and Thyrza had four children: Adeline Rebecca, born in 1823; Emily, in 1827; Henry, December 8, 1828, between eleven and twelve P.M.; and Edyth Caroline, in 1835.[5] His father recorded in his daybook that Henry was vaccinated on January 27, 1829; that on February 5 he was taken to the farm at Parker's Ferry; that on February 13 he was "sick (catarrh)" and on the 15th was "conval[escent]." The daybooks until 1836 have been lost, so there are no more even of these brief entries to be cited. Few stories survive of their family life, but Emily's daughter has recorded one: "When Henry Timrod was a little boy of four years he was standing at the window in their home in Charleston watching an electric storm. He was intensely interested. Presently, he exclaimed with a rapt look on his countenance, 'Mama, God is opening His great mouth and listen to His voice as it comes forth!' His father . . . , who was standing by, heard the little fellow. 'Thyrza,' he exclaimed, 'that boy will, if he lives, be a poet.'"[6]

In these years William Henry Timrod continued his trade of bookbinder. Hayne has described his shop: "Lawyers, editors, politicians, *litterateurs,* and gentlemen of scholarly ease and culture, would gather about his place of work, chiefly for the delight of listening to his unpremeditated and eloquent conversation. He seems indeed to have been—*longo intervallo*—a provincial Coleridge, holding his little audiences spell-bound by the mingled audacity and originality of his remarks." He also continued to write poetry. Perhaps the most attractive one is the simple-structured poem "To Harry," in which he hopes that childish mirth may endure but predicts a "full share of misery" for the boy. He seems to have been proudest of an anti-nullification ode, "Sons of the Union." It was a campaign poem, written during the violent controversy of 1832-33, and in bitterly unreserved lines it pleads for the preservation of freedom and of the Union. He also worked on and apparently completed a five-act drama which he regarded as "the literary labor of his life," but by "some strange fatality the manuscript of this play was lost—a misfortune which his son continually and bitterly lamented." [7]

In 1813 William had joined the German Friendly Society; in 1826, the German Fusiliers. He became Captain in 1834, and two years later he led his fifty-two volunteers, with another company of thirty also under his command, to St. Augustine, then threatened and to some degree under siege by the Seminole Indians. He was convinced that "Our arrival in Augustine saved that city, which otherwise would have afforded an easy prey to the savage foe. This was all I had in view and having effected it, I am more than satisfied." But he suffered from swamp fever and then from tuberculosis; after his return to Charleston, he resigned his commission on September 7, 1836, and accepted a job as inspector in the Custom House on the first of October, although he continued to do bookbinding in his spare time. He died on July 28, 1838. [8]

II *Boyhood*

By 1836, Henry was attending the small school run by the German Friendly Society, for on July 27 William cryptically recorded two items in his daybook: "Hallucanation pd. Harry's school to date." On November 7 he again paid the school fee, although he does not mention the amount. But the records of the society indicate that it had only one teacher who was employed at the rate of ten dollars per pupil quarterly. The school was not prospering, for in 1833 it had sold most of its equipment, and the one master was forced to teach English, German, Arithmetic, Latin, Greek, Pneumatics, and Electricity. The schoolroom was the hall of the Society, and the pupils were occasionally subjected to public examination by the members. [9]

Timrod soon transferred to the Classical School run by an English ex-army officer, Christopher Cotes (or Coates, as it was frequently spelled). This was the most celebrated school in Charleston. Cotes limited the number of students to one hundred, and he charged one hundred dollars a year tuition. In return, he offered a thorough course in the classics and in mathematics, and French taught by a native Frenchman. The school had one notable defect: Mr. Cotes did not like oratory; he refused to stress it, or to teach elocution. But he did not neglect rhetoric, history, logic, or ethics. Timrod became an outstanding Latin scholar, but he seems to have been only ordinarily proficient in his other studies.[10]

Paul Hamilton Hayne had the seat next to Timrod's; for a year, at least, Basil L. Gildersleeve, later a famous classical scholar, was a schoolmate. Mr. Cotes, or more probably his Yankee assistant, William E. Bailey, did not approve of poetry as an extracurricular exercise—at least, not when the verses were brought into the classroom. Late in life, when Hayne wrote the *Memoir,* he noted:

> I well remember the exultation with which he [Timrod] showed me, one morning, his earliest consecutive attempt at verse-making. It was a ballad of stirring adventures, and sanguinary catastrophe. But I thought it perfect—wonderful—and so, naturally, did he. Our "down East" schoolmaster, however, (all whose duties except those connected with penal inflictions, were left to his ushers, for our Principal united the morals of Pecksniff with the learning of Squeers), could boast of no turn for sentiment, and having remarked us hobnobbing, meanly assaulted us in the rear, effectually quenching for the time all *aesthetic enthusiasm.*[11]

A more sympathetic teacher described Henry Timrod as "diffident, modest, with a nervous utterance, yet with melody ever in his thoughts, and on his lips." His closest friend, Hayne, remembered him as

> Shy, but neither melancholy nor morose, he was passionate, impulsive, eagerly ambitious, with a thirst for knowledge hard to satiate. But too close a devotion to books did not destroy the natural lightness and simplicity of youth. He mingled freely with his comrades, all of whom respected, while some dearly loved him. At that time of life he was physically active and vigorous, and delighted in every sort of rough out-door sport; in leaping, running, wrestling, swimming, and even in *fighting.* More than once I have known him to engage in a desperate *affaire d'honneur,* the issue of which was decided by a primitive species of science that would have disgusted the orthodox "ring."[12]

Another associate, Bruns, presents a picture of a more solitary, withdrawn boy, who liked to go off by himself and who "rejoiced in the weekly holiday, with its long rambles through field and wood! And this taste strengthened with his growth. 'The sweet

security of streets,' that Elia loved, had no charm for him. . . .
Face to face with Nature he had no fears, no misgivings; always
a beneficent mother, she 'nursed him with the milk of a better
time,' and through all his years he leaned on her breast with the
loving trustfulness of a little child." [13] Henry's mother shared
this enthusiasm to such an extent that Emily wrote: "It was from
her, more than from his gifted father, that my brother (Henry
Timrod) derived his intense, passionate love of Nature." [14]

He continued to write poetry. What is said to be his earliest
extant poem, written at the age of fifteen, is a three-stanza
schoolboy's parody of Charles Wolfe's "The Burial of Sir John
Moore." In rollicking lines he commemorates the death of a tutor:

> Not a grin was seen, not a giggle heard
> As the tutor breath'd his last
> Not a Freshman uttered a jesting word
> At the thought of labours past.

However, a poem which he dated a year earlier, "In Bowers of
Ease," draws upon Thomson's "Castle of Indolence." [15] But the
influence of Moore and Byron, although less directly revealed, was
far more pervasive, and that of Wordsworth and Milton deeper
and more profoundly felt.

Some of the early poems were satiric; many years afterward
Henry T. Thompson remembered one that Timrod scribbled
in his copy of Cooper's Virgil:

> Behold the youth whose mighty mind
> Leaves all competitors behind!
> He translates Latin, thinks in Greek
> Well-nigh as fast as one can speak.[16]

Thompson and Bruns concur that Henry's favorite poets
among the classics were Virgil, Horace, and Catullus; there is
a tradition that he prepared for publication a translation, now
lost, of the lyrics of Catullus. Certainly his surviving copy of
Catullus is extensively annotated, revealing an interest in poetic
metaphor, in idiomatic expression, in variant readings suggested
by commentaries, and in identifying persons and places, especially the Greek and Latin synonyms for the same name.
Although he read Greek easily, there is no discernible influence;
Hayne notes that "the horror and gloom" of Aeschylean drama
revolted Timrod, but that "sad Electra's poet" charmed him.[17]

III *College Days*

Some of this knowledge may have been acquired later. In January, 1845, he entered the University of Georgia at the beginning of the second term. He was admitted as an irregular student, probably because he entered in the middle of the school year, but he was apparently better prepared than most students, for he was assigned to the sophomore class as a matriculate of 1847, and assigned also to Room 31 in the New College dormitory. He paid fees in January and August, 1845, and in January, 1846; since no other entries appeared in his name in extant university records, there seems no reason to doubt that before August, 1846, he had quitted the University.

If as a second-term sophomore Timrod followed the required curriculum, he had courses in Horace, Sophocles, Euclid, History, and French, followed the third term by Juvenal, Euripides, Logarithms, Plane Trigonometry, Mensuration, Botany, and Application of Algebra to Geometry. As a first-term Junior he presumably studied Surveying, Navigation, Natural Philosophy, and Homer's *Iliad;* the next term Conic Sections, Spherical Geometry and Trigonometry, Natural Philosophy, Rhetoric, and Cicero's *De Oratore.* The final term, which he may not have completed, prescribed Differential and Integral Calculus, Natural Philosophy, Moral Philosophy, Chemistry, and Logic. Since no record of grades or class standing seems to have survived, it is impossible to be certain just what courses Timrod had, or how he fared in them.

The only other record available is in the carelessly kept Minutes of the Demosthenian Society. On June 14, 1845, Timrod was elected Door-keeper; probably he had joined this literary and debating society soon after he entered college. A week later, he was impeached for having been absent for three successive meetings, but his excuse was accepted. On September 11, he was elected to deliver the society's eulogy on a recently deceased classmate, and two days later he "detained the house for a few moments with some eloquent and pathetic remarks." In January, 1846, he was elected Clerk of the Tribunal; in February appointed to the Committee on Questions; and in March (after once being excused) he gave a Junior Oration and entertained the audience with "chaste and eloquent remarks." This is the last official record of Timrod's connection with the University of Georgia. Hayne and other friends attributed his leaving to temporary ill health and to financial difficulties.[18]

Certain extracurricular activities appear to have interested him more than his classes. There is an unsubstantiated but plausible tradition that he sometimes drank more than was considered seemly; there is no doubt that he spent much time with young ladies, and perhaps even more in writing poems to or about them. According to Hayne, Timrod laughingly told him that a large part " 'of my leisure at college, was occupied in the composition of love verses, frantic or tender. Every pretty girl's face I met acted upon me like an inspiration!' . . . Some of the cleverest of these love-songs were published in *The Charleston Evening News,* over a fictitious signature. They became, *locally,* quite popular, and in one instance, to the author's intense delight, his verses were set to music." Unfortunately, this pseudonym continues to elude identification, but one of his sonnets, signed T. H., appeared in the Charleston *Evening News* as early as September 8, 1846, and a lyric, "Eyes," on September 16.[19]

A typical early poem, dated October, 1845 and in a stanzaic form borrowed from Burns, beyond question belongs to his university days:

What Athens Dull

What Athens dull thou maudlin rake
If ten long faces once could make
A city safe as Moses spake,
    I can't tell where,
When threaten'd loud with fire and flake
    For badness sair,

Sure then some three of the bonniest lasses
With winsome forms and gleesome faces
As e'er spurn'd artful paints or laces
    To make their beauty
A second trio o' the graces
    Should teach your duty.

Several of the poems dated in this period are written to young ladies given such plausible names as Marie, Isabel, and Cousin Lou; one is to a pastorally named Chloe; but the greater number are addressed to unidentified and generalized girls. One poem that is easily identifiable is a clever acrostic to Anne Waddel, the daughter of a professor and the granddaughter of a president of the University of Georgia. Probably this same young lady is pictured in a highly fanciful poem as receiving from Cupid all his powers, bestowing them on "Anne's frown . . . and laughing eye." But however freely his fancy may have roamed, Timrod seems to have left Athens with his heart intact.[20]

IV *Youthful Poet*

In the best tradition of impecunious Southern gentlemen, Timrod, after his return to Charleston, read law in the office of one of Charleston's ablest and most stern-minded men, James L. Petigru. He was not happy in this apprenticeship. Years later, Judge George S. Bryan wrote to Hayne that

> Timrod was too wholly a poet to keep company long with so relentless, rugged, and exacting a mistress as the law! As a curious illustration of the abstraction and reverie which so often absorbed the poet, he told me that Mr. Petigru sent him on one occasion to take a message to a certain Factor on the Bay. But as ill-luck would have it, when he had gone half way he found he had forgotten, if indeed he ever really knew, the message entrusted to his care. What was to be done? He could only return, and, with as bold a face as possible, acknowledged his misfortune.
>
> On his doing so, Mr. Petigru saluted him, very much excited, in his highest squeaking voice, *"Why, Harry, you are a fool!"* And, added our poet friend to me, "I would have been a fool to Mr. Petigru to the end of my days, even had I revealed in after-life the genius of a Milton or a Shakespeare!" [21]

Timrod's close friend Dr. John Dickson Bruns described him as being, in these prewar years, ". . . below the medium height. He had always excelled in boyish sports and as he grew to manhood his great breadth of shoulder still seemed to indicate physical vigor which the shallow chest, the slender waist, the thin transparent hands and habitually lax attitude but too plainly contradicted. His hair, which was very dark, fell in loose masses over a low but broad forehead. The square jaw was almost stern, the mouth large, the lips exquisitely sensitive, the grey eyes set deep under heavy brows." Sometime in these years he added to his dark, romantic appearance by growing a heavy black moustache.[22]

Various friends have testified to his quick and nervous walk, his tendency to stammer under strain, his shyness and reserve among strangers, his diffidence and his occasional impulsiveness, his poverty followed by extravagance the few times that he had money. He was high-strung, easily offended, and often melancholy; William Gilmore Simms, in fact, thought that "His temperament was morbid. . . . Give him a good condition, under any circumstance, and this temperament would always work to his discomfort and disquietude. His hope was small. He had none of the sanguine in his system." Timrod's sister Emily, however, bitterly labeled this as false: "Never was a more unjust estimate of character . . . so very little made him happy." Both Hayne and Bruns testify to his droll humor and add that, when he returned to Charleston, he would be "welcomed by a small coterie of friends with demonstrative cordiality." [23]

After abandoning legal study, Timrod returned to the classics, with the vain hope that by private study he could fit himself for a college professorship. He continued to write poetry, and by 1849 he was publishing identifiable poems under the pen-name "Aglaus"—the name of a minor Greek pastoral poet. The earliest lyrics appeared in the *Southern Literary Messenger*, but he was soon publishing in Charleston newspapers and in the *Southern Literary Gazette*. By 1856 he had dropped the pseudonym; although he published a few poems anonymously, he nearly always signed his work with his name or initials.[24]

The coterie mentioned by Hayne frequently met in the rooms of the Charleston Mechanics' Library Association to read poetry aloud or to engage in informal debates. Notable among them were Timrod, Hayne, Bruns, Gildersleeve (until he left to study in Germany), Eugene Baker, and John della Torre. Della Torre, an accomplished Latinist, pulled a joke quite typical of the time. One of Timrod's poems had been published in the Charleston *Mercury;* della Torre translated it into Latin and wrote the translation on the fly-leaf of a book of medieval Latin lyrics. Bruns then accused Timrod of plagiarism, and della Torre, concealing the page, read aloud the Latin version of Timrod's own poem. The bewildered Timrod professed ignorance of the verses: "I am astonished by the extraordinary similarity of the verses, and it would seem to prove what I have long wildly dreamed, that there is truth in metempsychosis, and that in some previous state of existence I was the Latin poet myself." After feigning incredulity, the friends admitted the hoax—to Timrod's considerable relief.[25]

Early in the 1850's, according to Hayne, this younger group was absorbed into a larger group that met frequently but informally in a comfortable back room in John Russell's bookshop or at Simms's town house, which he called the "Wigwam." The younger men regarded Simms as the leader: "it is not wonderful that he should have gathered around him, through the forces of sympathy and genius, a number of ambitious young men, who enjoyed his conversation, deferred to his judgment, and regarded him in literary matters as a guide, philosopher, and friend!" The older men showed little deference. Notable among them were the staunch Unionist, James L. Petigru, as famous for his after-dinner *mots* as for his legal knowledge; Samuel Henry Dickson, professor in the Medical College, author of numerous scientific and literary essays, and of graceful occasional poems; Alfred Huger and Mitchell King, equally noted as able scholars and brilliant lawyers; the professor of German, August Sachtleben; the learned Roman Catholic priest, Father Lynch (later a bishop); the mystical Protestant, James W. Miles, author of *Philosophic Theology* (1849), and his younger brother, William Porcher Miles; and William J. Grayson, lawyer, author of *The Hireling and the Slave* (1854), and devoted adherent of neoclassicism and of Dryden and Pope. Three of the younger men, Basil Gildersleeve, David Ramsay, and Samuel Lord, were graduates of the University of Göttingen.[26]

As writers, all were amateurs except Simms, and no doubt most of them were far better as conversationalists than as essayists and poets. No doubt, also, Simms was correct when he proclaimed orally and in magazines that only rarely was amateur writing likely to be good writing; that, if Charleston ever produced a sound body of worthwhile literature, it would be primarily by trained, hardworking professionals. But at least there was literary and philosophical excitement, even though it was subordinate to political and legal matters; there was an interest in discussing ideas, and in meeting with Sachtleben to read Goethe and Schiller in German; there was the sharpening attrition of mind on mind.[27]

V *Tutor*

Timrod's attendance at these informal meetings was intermittent. Poverty forced him, when he failed to secure a university professorship, to accept tutorial positions on various plantations. This was, for the time, lucrative and not unpleasant work. A tutor usually became an added member of the family, taking his meals with them and being provided with a comfortable bedroom. The salary ranged from $600 to $1,000 a year in addition to room and board. The tutor frequently engaged in hunting and fishing and other family sports, although there is no record that Timrod did so; he seems to have preferred solitary rambles in the woods. Often the owner would build a small schoolhouse for his own and sometimes his neighbors' children, though one suspects that this may have been to remove the noise of the students from the house rather than to protect the students from household distractions. In return, the tutor was expected to prepare the boys for college. This meant a reasonably thorough grounding in Greek, Latin, Mathematics, and Rhetoric, with some attention to Philosophy, Ethics, and Logic. For the girls, French was normally substituted for Greek, although there is evidence in Timrod's "Præceptor Amat" that he read Homer in the original with his favorite pupil, Felicia Robinson.[28]

According to Henry T. Thompson, a somewhat unreliable biographer, Timrod's first tutorial position was on the plantation, near Charleston, of a Mr. Lowndes. This had the advantage of allowing Timrod more frequent access to his friends and more participation in literary affairs, but this proximity also offered temptations. Apparently the pay was good, for Timrod one day went to Charleston with $300 in his pocket. The next day Lowndes met a disconsolate tutor, who confessed: "Like a fool, I have squandered my last dollar,—my idiotic soul! literally thrown it away,—my idiotic soul!" After this drinking and gambling spree, Timrod threatened to join the Order of the Rechabites, but was easily dissuaded.[29]

By July 4, 1851, Timrod was tutoring in the family of Daniel

Blake, the son and the grandson of distinguished and wealthy Carolinians. Timrod's letter to Emily was written from Buncombe County, North Carolina, and Blake is reputed to have been the first South Carolinian to have built a summer home in the mountains near Asheville. Timrod may have been on Blake's low country plantation of "Combahee" the winter before. The evidence is confusing. In July he wrote: "I see some very beautiful scenery, and now and then meet some very pleasant people. . . . If I have not forgotten Charleston and its attachments,—at least—I begin to appreciate Buncombe better. . . . Mr. and Mrs. Blake profess to be much pleased with me." This sounds as though he were in a new position, especially when he adds that he is pleased with the Blakes, and that Mrs. Blake had called his French pronunciation "elegant." But on October 3 he wrote to Emily that "In six or seven weeks I shall be in Charleston, though how long to stay I don't know. Mr. Blake, I think, expects me to go with him to Combahee. This will be altogether against my inclinations, but if he prefers me, Lord knows whether I shall say no. Yet I am half mad when I think of spending another winter on a low country plantation."

Apparently he remained with the Blakes through the summer of 1853, for on July 29 he wrote Emily: "Pray since you have made Chapman's acquaintance, tell him I should be very glad to meet him in Buncombe again." Possibly the mountains in summer compensated for the plantation in winter. Two years earlier he had enthusiastically described the comfortable house built on a pleasant plateau surrounded by mountains; the eminence near the house that had been leveled to make a spacious garden "laid out much in the English fashion"; the cool climate that made even the rains pleasant; and, above all, the pleasant walks through the surrounding woods. With even more enthusiasm he described an aurora borealis as "the most astonishing and beautiful spectacle I have ever seen." [30]

Before April, 1856, Timrod was a tutor in the plantation home of Murray Robinson, near Rowesville in Orangeburg County. This was his favorite of all the tutorial positions that he held: "These woods and grounds seem to help me to think." Felicia Robinson was his favorite pupil, even though on one occasion she threatened to be "a real Saracen Omar/To a certain much-valued edition of Homer." Poetically at least he fancied

himself halfway in love with her, as he indicates in his play-
fully Browningesque poem, "Præceptor Amat."

In turn, Felicia has left a sympathetic and graphic description
of her tutor:

> I remember Mr. Timrod well, with all the pleasant impressions
> of childhood. With us he was like a member of our family, mak-
> ing himself such by his unobtrusive, gentle nature, and by the
> deep interest which he always took in our affairs. He was very
> considerate, sympathetic and affectionate in disposition. I have
> heard him spoken of as a "crank," which is unjust. He was very
> absent-minded, and was often so absorbed in poetical fancies
> that he would appear peculiar. He spent as much of his time
> as his duties would allow in reading and studying, and was
> rarely without some book in his hand. Tennyson and Wordsworth
> were his favorites, I think as he carried old worn copies in his
> pockets. He was a very learned man, being devoted to the
> classics, and able to read fluently French, German, Latin and
> Greek.

This tendency to lapse into reverie was not displeasing to his
pupils, although he might suddenly start up and say, "Now
begin!" [31]

In 1857 Timrod visited his favorite sister Emily at Mars Bluff,
in what is now Florence County, South Carolina. Emily had
married an Englishman, George Munro Goodwin; after he met
with business reverses in Charleston, he moved to the Pee Dee
region to become plantation overseer, storekeeper, and book-
keeper for Colonel William Henry Cannon. For the Goodwins,
Colonel Cannon built a white frame house, "Forest Cottage";
when he prevailed upon Henry Timrod to teach his and some
of his neighbors' children, Colonel Cannon built for him a
twelve by fifteen-foot frame schoolhouse. The tiny schoolhouse,
turned into a Timrod museum with a few of his books in it,
is now four miles from the Cannon plantation, on the Central
School grounds in Florence, South Carolina.

The next year, Mr. Goodwin's father and his sister Kate came
from England for what proved to be a permanent visit. For a
school year, Timrod taught his future wife, but one of Colonel
Cannon's daughters later wrote that "Kate Goodwin, whom he
also taught at this time, was about eighteen years of age. Timrod
scarcely noticed her then." [32]

Timrod had reluctantly accepted the place. In Charleston there had been a renewed outburst of literary enthusiasm. In 1856, in the comfortable back room of Russell's bookshop, a group of men had decided to establish a magazine. Simms had made the *Southern Quarterly Review* an important political and critical journal, but he had held strictly to the concept that it was a review, not a magazine; and he had the year before given up the editorship, with the result that the *Review* was moved to Columbia. But these men wanted an entirely different kind of periodical; they desired to establish a monthly literary magazine that would be representative "not merely of local, but of *Southern* intellect, taste, and opinion," and that would be hospitable to Northern authors. John Russell had, "after much natural hesitation, agreed, with a reckless gallantry I have always admired, to undertake the publication and entire business management of the work, and to 'foot all bills' not covered by an exceedingly limited subscription list." As a minor and unremunerative recompense, it was appropriately named *Russell's Magazine*.[33]

Timrod had helped to plan the magazine, and he was enthusiastic about its prospects. His closest friend, Paul Hamilton Hayne, accepted the editorship; but Timrod felt that he could not take an active position on the staff because of his lengthy but necessary absences from Charleston. Also, his latent tuberculosis had become active; and Emily, using his illness as a persuasive force, argued that the up country was more healthful than the moist Charleston region and that at Mars Bluff he could have expert medical treatment from Dr. Edward Porcher. Timrod was forced to be only a contributor, although he was not quite content with the position.[34]

The first issue of *Russell's* appeared in April, 1857, and it included Timrod's poem "The Arctic Voyager." In the three years of the magazine's life, hardly an issue appeared without a Timrod poem in it, and sometimes Hayne published three or four of Timrod's poems in the same month, with some of them appearing anonymously. Hayne was a partisan editor, consistently praising and publishing the works of his friends Timrod, Simms, and W. J. Grayson, but he attempted to make the magazine lively and representative. So he accepted delightedly a serial by the Virginian John Esten Cooke, and was mortified when he could not pay the agreed-upon price. Of Northern writers he remembered with especial pleasure John W. De Forest, "who sent me an inimitable sketch, brimming over with fun, entitled, 'The Smartville Ram Speculation'; and Richard Henry Stoddard, whose 'Herod Agrippa and the Owl' deserves to rank with the best of his blank-verse poems." [35]

Some of the articles have the quality of oral argument, or of debate. One of the bookshop regulars attacked dueling, and another defended it. Timrod's first prose contribution was a short essay, "The Character and Scope of the Sonnet," [36] but his second article was a rebuttal, which he had already made orally. In the July, 1857, issue Hayne published an article that Timrod disagreed with almost completely: W. J. Grayson's "What is Poetry?" It was the work of a man who admired Dryden and Pope, but who was totally unsympathetic with the ideas and the works of the Romantic poets. Grayson argued that poetry is simply verse, regardless of whether it is good or bad. Timrod indignantly denied this, maintaining that poetry has its own language and that, however abstract his thought, "the poet is compelled, by his passion-fused imagination, to give it life, form, or color." Unfortunately Timrod's article had the same title as Grayson's, with the chaotic result that Timrod is frequently quoted as saying what he was fervently denying. [37]

In 1859 Timrod published a third critical article in *Russell's*, although it appears to have been written first as a lecture. "Literature in the South" is a thoughtful assessment of the difficulties besetting the Southern author in a region without publishers and among a people who "know Pope and Horace by heart, but who have never read a word of Wordsworth or Tennyson, or who have read them with suspicion, and rejected them with superciliousness." He pleaded that international critical standards should replace nationalistic or sectional partisanship, that Southern readers recognize native genius and above all understand "that most important revolution in imaginative literature—to us of the present day the most important of all literary revolutions—which took place a little more than half a century ago." At a time when the emphasis was still on Greek and Latin, Timrod advocated that colleges should teach English literature. [38]

From the work which he had published in the *Southern*

Literary Messenger, Russell's, and various Charleston news-papers, Timrod in 1859 selected enough poems to fill out a small volume; it was published, apparently by subscription, by Ticknor and Fields of Boston. The book was available in Charleston a few days before Christmas, 1859, but nationally it got only a few reviews, and the one edition had not been exhausted at the time of Timrod's death. He was proud of his book, but, like many another poet, vexed at its poor reception and poorer sales. His friend Bruns wrote after his death: "He had hoped, earnestly and justly, to make a little rift through which the light of popular favor might steal, and now only clouds and shadows were closing round him." [39]

A book of poems and numerous contributions to a non-paying magazine were not enough to support him or to contribute to the support of his mother. Tutorial work, as he had discovered, was likely to be temporary. Students grew up, parents became dissatisfied, or the tutor himself grew weary of the same faces. On May 7, 1860, he started work as a teacher in the school at Bluffton, South Carolina, of which Hugh L. Train was Principal. By the next day, Timrod regretted his decision:

> If I could have anticipated the task before me, nothing could have induced me to accept the situation. If I had sought the world over for the place most unsuited to my tastes and habits, I could not have succeeded anywhere as well as I have here. . . . I began school yesterday; and the boys set straightaway to see of what stuff I was made. Some of them being young men, were inclined to put on airs, but I met every demonstration with a promptness and decision which astonished them very soon into proper behaviour. I think they were already satisfied that in my department I intend to be autocrat, independently even of Mr. Train.
>
> Still all of this is disagreeable to me who have always been accustomed to make my pupils my companions. Of course, in a large school like this, it will be impossible to do anything of the sort. . . . To tell the plain truth, however, I was not born to be a teacher, and I expect with my inordinate sensibility to encounter much that will give me acute pain. If I could fling up the situation honourably, I would do so at once, and I am positive that I will not teach after the expiration of this year. If I can't get a professorship, I must see whether I can't live on a poet's pittance.[40]

Although he was resolved to "face my fate bravely" and was somewhat consoled because he had been given "an arithmetical class of little girls, one or two of whom are sweet and very interesting," he felt that he was too depressed to "say anything of interest." G. A. Wauchope relates a plausible if unsubstantiated story that differs from Timrod's and may help to explain his discontent. That first day, the school bully refused to obey his smaller teacher. Timrod, according to regulations, reported the incident to the principal, who insisted upon personally meting out punishment. After school was out, the bully armed himself with a stick and hid in some bushes along the road; as Timrod passed, the bully came out and threatened him with "the ——est thrashing now that you ever heard of." The suspicious principal had followed Timrod, and he thundered at the boy, "You are right, sir, there is going to be the ——est thrashing you ever heard of, but you are the scoundrel that's going to get it!" The incident is unimportant, in a time when the older boys constantly tested a new master; yet it is also significant. Timrod was not a disciplinarian. He could not impose his will upon several classes mixed together in one room, or compete with the noise of students studying aloud. After the term ended, he returned to private tutoring.[41]

In the meantime, he had come to like Bluffton, its people, and its scenery. Dr. Guerard took him riding in his buggy and treated him when he was ill; various persons invited him to dinner, or sent a carriage so that he might have an afternoon ride. Although he did not refuse to be sociable, he remained solitary: "My usual afternoon's exercise, however, is a walk on the bluff, or through the woods behind Bluffton." He reported to Emily that "the pain in my chest is decreasing daily."[42]

VI *Early Loves*

The young poet and tutor may scarcely have noticed Katie Goodwin, but he was not unmindful of other girls. After the Goodwins moved to Columbia in November, 1859, Timrod frequently visited them. There he met and fell in love with Sophie Sosnowski. His feeling that marriage with her was an unattainable goal increased his discontent with being in Bluffton; from there he sent her "a third version of my endless poem" about her. In its published form, "Two Portraits" is hardly as much a love poem as a tribute to her womanliness: Timrod contrasted a girl who declared she would remain single with the fulfillment that she would find as wife and mother. The poem did not convince her. Before June 11, 1860, the courtship had ended abruptly. Henry wrote his sister that Sophie had mortified him by speaking lightly of his passion and by telling him to "be a man." Timrod was especially hurt by this accusation: "I have generally been held to be a man by those who know me." Yet he continued to value her friendship, and he did not completely give up the courtship until a year later, when he wrote that he had no longer any hope and apologized for certain events that had made him "determined to be pure and temperate." [43]

This failure in love was at least partially compensated by a new interest. Timrod had met a witty and strikingly beautiful brunette, Rachel Lyons. She became for him "La Belle Juive," and under that title he wrote for her one of his best love poems. When he presented her with a copy of his one book, he wrote on the flyleaf a poem which he signed H. T.:

To R. L.

I had not looked upon your face
　　When these poor songs were penned,
And therefore, could not catch the grace
　　Which charms like yours would lend.

Whence, haply, if you find at times
　　Some verse too feebly wrought,
A pardon for its faltering rhymes
　　Accord with this sweet thought:

"How perfect would have been his art,
　　His strains how deep and strong,
If Rachel then had filled his heart,
　　And Rachel fired his song!"

Essentially, however, this relationship seems to have been a stimulating literary friendship rather than a courtship, and it continued to flourish in letters after Timrod in January, 1861, accepted a tutorship in the Joseph Hazel family at Hardeeville, South Carolina, to prepare young Hazel for college. [44]

The situation and the people were neither good nor bad: "I

am among very good people, but far plainer and less pretending than the Blufftonians. I must say too that I prefer a little more polish than I have seen yet; but I am ready to overlook the absence of that in consideration of the really sterling qualities which supply its place." The situation did not improve as the months passed, and Timrod was pleased when, in June, "Young Hazel having relinquished his intention of going to college, I am at liberty to do as I please. I am sick of the place and the people—the Hazels, who are very kind and dull people, being excepted. Would you believe it, that though only sixteen miles from Bluffton, I have never been able to get a conveyance to take me thither. The Hazels might oblige me, but as they know my desire to visit my friends of last summer, and yet have never offered to assist me, I can't stoop to ask them." These disadvantages were counterbalanced by the fact that no other place was open. So Timrod stayed on, working desultorily with his uninterested pupil, and requesting Emily to send him in her next letter "a little blood and thunder, mixed with original allusions to the Palmetto flag; and then perhaps I may write a song worthy of the occasion and—the people." [45]

Timrod was roused to poetic and patriotic fervor by the meeting of the Confederate Congress in Montgomery, Alabama, and by the prospect that the South would become an independent nation. In February, 1861, he wrote "Ethnogenesis," and the next month he read the poem aloud in Charleston, before it was published as a broadside. But he found life in Hardeeville dull, and insufficiently leavened by infrequent visits to Columbia and Charleston. He wrote to Rachel Lyons that "I purpose being very poetical this summer (if the Yankees leave us unmolested)." He expanded on this in a later letter:

I shall be so utterly alone for the next few months, that I shall be compelled for mere lack of employment, to betake myself to rhyming. At present I am casting about for a subject on which to string my fancies, but as yet have failed to satisfy my (perhaps) somewhat too fastidious Muse. There is one theme indeed (An Arctic Voyage) which has haunted me from childhood; but as it is on my treatment of that theme that I wish to stake my hopes of a lasting fame, I shall put off the execution of it until my powers, such as they are, shall have attained their utmost strength, which I do not think they have done yet. [46]

VII   *War Poet*

In July Timrod joined, with the proviso that he could resign if he left the district, a military company which had been raised for the defense of the Beaufort coast, and he was elected quartermaster, secretary, and treasurer. He resigned as tutor and soldier in September, 1861, and returned to Charleston. He had completed a sonnet, "I know not why," which he said illustrated "the dark moods which have not seldom visited me during this infernal summer." He had also written one of his longest, most ambitious, and most patriotically optimistic odes, "The Cotton Boll," which he intended to publish "in the paper which I think will pay me the highest price." He took with him also "the skeletons" of several poems, but he was not optimistic about them: "The lyre of Tyrtaeus is the only one to which the Public will listen now; and over that martial instrument I have but small command."

His next considerable poems were, in fact, tributes to young ladies. He wrote to Rachel Lyons that "The Goddess knocked at the door of my study last Saturday night and handed me a poem entitled 'Katie'! I have sent it to the *Mercury* in the columns of which it will probably appear on Friday. . . . I am more anxious that this poem should be liked than I have ever been in regard to any other I have written." In January, 1862, he sent Miss Lyons a poetic tribute entitled "Rachel," but for publication he changed the title to "La Belle Juive."

Although his friends "tried to dissuade . . . [him] from going into the war," on the reasonable ground that his "pen is too valuable a one to be risked," Timrod before March 1, 1862, enlisted in the 30th South Carolina Regiment, commanded by his friend, Colonel Lawrence M. Keitt. Earlier, if he would have enlisted as a gentleman volunteer, Keitt had promised him a horse and the dignity, but not the rank or the pay, of an officer. Timrod had felt that he was too poor to accept this somewhat noncommittal position. Slightly over a month after he enlisted and before he had gone to the camp on James Island, Keitt got him appointed as regimental clerk. Certainly he was qualified for this essential though unmilitary chore, but Keitt was basically attempting to protect the health of his tubercular friend.[47]

In fact, as Timrod indicated to Emily in his letter of February

25, 1862, he thought the citizens of Charleston unduly optimistic. It was impossible "to persuade Ma and Rebecca to leave the city at present." And matters looked "ugly in the West," with Northern gunboats in control of the rivers. The main hope, "as I heard a man say last night with some force and a little irreverence," was that "Beauregard and a Confederate God will save us in the issue." Earlier Timrod had been confident that England would intervene, but in words anticipatory of Frank Owsley, Avery Craven, Vann Woodward, and other modern historians, and in denial of his own poem, he wrote that "We have overrated the power of King Cotton. When King Wheat gets upon his throne, he is just as strong." As it turned out, wheat was stronger; but Timrod, a bewildered man in his own economic world, may have been the first to realize why England could not afford to support the Confederacy.

Timrod's regimental clerkship was a sinecure, but for that reason it was boring. Moreover, he had become engaged to Katie Goodwin; and on April 11, 1862, he wrote to his sister Emily: "I set off tomorrow night for Corinth as the war correspondent of the *Mercury*. The terms of my engagement are very advantageous—higher even than Personne's with the *Courier*. I get six dollars a day, and my traveling expenses paid." He had letters of introduction to Beauregard and to members of his staff. Timrod arrived in time to take part in the Confederate retreat from Shiloh; as Hayne wrote of Timrod's experience, "Out of the refluent tides of blood, from under the smoke of conflict, the sickening fumes of slaughter, he staggered homeward, half blinded, bewildered, with a dull mist before his eyes, and a shuddering horror at heart." John Dickson Bruns added that "the story of his camp life would furnish a theme for mirth, if our laughter were not choked by tears."

Unable to endure the rigors and hardships of camp life, Timrod made his way to Mobile. There he was occasionally entertained in the home of the author and social leader Octavia Le Vert; there he met James Ryder Randall, author of "Maryland, My Maryland." In 1899 Randall wrote of their association:

> Many years ago, when we were both quite young, I met Timrod in Mobile. He was essaying the difficult role of war correspondent, but his mind was unfitted for such rude employment and "dwelt among the stars." He could hardly travel any dis-

tance without losing his valise; and he had that singular disease which makes one blind or nearly so at night. I had to carry him around, at dusk, as if he were sightless. Even in those days he was extremely fragile and a manifest victim of consumption. Yet he strove vigorously to combat with a world for which he was not robustly fitted and whose sordid objects were somewhat contemptible and unworthy.[48]

VIII *Poet of Peace*

One notable result of this experience was that partisanship almost disappeared from Timrod's poetry. Only when Charleston was threatened with invasion did he rouse himself to martial ardor, and even this poem ends on a note of stoic fatalism:

> . . . in the temple of the fates
> God has inscribed her doom;
> And, all untroubled in her faith, she waits
> The triumph or the tomb.
> *(Poems,* 148)

This fatalism was far removed from his earlier optimism. Henceforth, to him war was evil, regardless of who won or lost; it was the horror and the human waste of war that he emphasized.

Back in Charleston, in late July of 1862, Timrod debated with himself what to do. He regarded his future as "altogether uncertain. I am advised by my physician not to return to camp, but in the absence of all employment, what else can I do? My mind and body are both in too sickly a state for study, and I cannot consent, while so many better men than myself are enduring the hardships of a campaign, to 'lay on the roses, and feed on the lilies of life.' On the other hand I cannot help knowing that I could do but little service in the field." He did return to his military clerkship, but by October 28 he admitted that he was "totally unfit for camp" and was about to apply for a discharge. He was officially discharged from the Confederate Army on December 15, 1862, because of ill health.[49]

A new project, or at least possibility, excited him and absorbed his time and energy. Two Charleston friends, George A. Trenholm and Theodore D. Wagner, proposed that an illustrated English edition of his poems be published. An English artist, Frank Vizetelly, who was in Charleston as war correspondent of the London *News*, offered to do the illustrations and to arrange for the publication. Timrod collected those poems that he thought suitable, revised them, and had them set in type so that he might send perfect copies to the English printer. The project came to nothing. John R. Thompson, who also hoped to publish his own poems in London, thought that the work failed to get through the blockade; Hayne and Timrod's wife blamed it on "the hurry and pressure of great events"; on the ever-increasing bleakness as "the darkest days of the Confederacy fell upon us," especially in beleaguered Charleston; and on Trenholm's becoming Confederate Secretary of the Treasury, with no time "to give a thought to anything private." Timrod was bitterly disappointed; nearly two years later he wrote to Hayne: "The project of publishing my poems in England has been silently but altogether dropped. It *is* a disappointment, of course, but I grin and bear it, as the lot of a poor poet." [50]

He made one more attempt to serve in the army. After the Northern attack on Morris Island in July, 1863, he was so excited that he "went to enroll . . . in one of the companies which had volunteered for the defense of Charleston. Alas! I soon found my abilities unequal to my will; a day's service sufficed to convince me that I was unable to discharge the duties that I had undertaken. With a hemorrhage hardly stanched, I stated my case to my Captain, who at once counseled me to withdraw from the company. I do so, and am now once more a useless citizen. How very little the country will have owed me at the conclusion of this war." [51]

In August, 1863, Timrod became assistant editor of the Charleston *Mercury*. When he was in this position, William Gordon McCabe, Virginia poet and schoolmaster, met him and described him as "a small, melancholy-looking man, black moustache, grey eyes and sallow complexion. Very pleasant he is in conversation." According to McCabe's biographer, Timrod was a semi-invalid, and McCabe helped in preparing some of the articles for the paper before they discussed "literature and writers, especially Tennyson whom each admired." Timrod was not entirely pleased with the position, for it was not "the one best suited to my tastes and habits; but I am perfectly willing to do anything that will make me independent."

The new job would not do that, for it paid barely enough to

support him, so that it "will be a long time before I can think of that which makes the end of all my aspirations—marriage. I don't know how you would regard it; but to me the situation which I am now in—betrothed to a charming girl [Katie Goodwin] whom I love with all my heart, and whom it is notwithstanding, from the poverty of my circumstances impossible for me to marry—is a profound grief." Moreover, his newspaper duty was, he wrote, "that which in the Courier office is divided between two or more—to collect facts and to reduce them in form and proportions. In discharging the first task, I am afraid that I shall be very unskillful at first; and my reserve with strangers, which I have always found so difficult to overcome, will make it even a disagreeable labour. Nevertheless, I am determined to trample on every delicacy which may stand in my way." [52]

IX   *Editor*

Mainly through the financial aid of his friend Theodore Wagner, Timrod in January, 1864, became associate editor and a partner in the daily *South Carolinian,* published in Columbia. He resigned from the *Mercury* and left Charleston, although with some misgivings: "Wagner, in making conditions in my behalf, rated me at the usual rate which poets go for, and I was subordinate in pecuniary interest and therefore in practical authority not only to the senior editor, but to the head printer of the journal." This does not seem so unjust as Timrod thought it, for Timrod's partners were Felix Gregory De Fontaine, well-known as a war correspondent under the pen-name of Personne, and Julian A. Selby, an experienced printer and businessman. Timrod's first editorial appeared on January 13, 1864. [53]

Late in 1863 or early in 1864, Timrod delivered as a lecture in Columbia his most important critical essay. His widow wrote that she could not find the exact date, but "I am quite sure it was some time in 63—before we were married, but were engaged. It was given in aid of the poor soldiers who as you will well know were in a most deplorable condition, half starved, and half-clothed." [54]

Encouraged by his prospects, Timrod married Katie Goodwin on February 16, 1864. [55] At first Timrod seemed happy in his work and with his marriage. Simms visited him in May and wrote to Hayne that "I saw Timrod and was glad to find him in better health and spirits than he has had for years before." Simms credited this to temperance and employment and to the influence of a young wife whom he never met. Timrod was becoming a fine prose writer, and work on a daily newspaper would modify his tendency toward "the essayical." The energetic Simms added that the "labour is not exhaustive, nor very various. He has only to prepare a couple of dwarf essays, making a single column, and the pleasant public is satisfied. These he does so well, that they have reason to be so. Briefly, our friend is in a fair way to fatten, and be happy, though his muse becomes costive and complains of his *mésalliances*." [56]

Hayne was less easily convinced. In 1870 he remembered Katie as anything but a poet, by "nature, expression, or association. On the contrary (and I say this in strictest confidence) she is a trivial, foolish, shallow-brained, if not a bad-hearted woman,—who married Timrod, in a freak of disappointed vanity, —made his life, (though he never complained by word or deed), unhappy, and who, I understand upon good authority, is not likely in any way, to honor his memory!!"

Moreover, Timrod had written freely to Hayne of his business difficulties. His position was one of "far less dignity, power and profit than I think my due. The journal would be another, and, I flatter myself, a better thing, if it were my own." When Timrod wrote the notice of a book, De Fontaine took possession of it in spite of the custom that such books are "the perquisites of him who criticizes them." De Fontaine wrote the book notices, and to Timrod "One pleasant consequence of this is that his wretched criticisms are credited to me by the public, while all my leaders are attributed to him." De Fontaine also seized upon all the literary journals for his wife, who kept a file of them; and Timrod wrote that, if Hayne wished a poem republished from some other paper, "You must send it to me." Timrod, who was also disturbed when Clara Dargan wrote that he probably occupied the editorial chair during De Fontaine's absence as war correspondent, replied: "I have occupied that chair since it passed into the hands of Messrs. de Fontaine and Co. With the exception of about a dozen furnished by Mr. de Fontaine during my absence or temporary illness, I have written every leader and leading editorial that has appeared in the paper since January of this year. . . . I mention this not from any vanity— you will acquit me of that—but because it is of some pecuniary importance to me that the amount of labor which I have given to the Carolinian should be generally known." [57]

There were also personal troubles. In late August Katie was threatened with a miscarriage, and for several days Timrod felt uncertain as to what would happen. George Goodwin, frail for several years, seemed to be failing rapidly; Henry's youngest sister Edyth, wife of A. H. Cotchett, was also sick. There were also literary vexations. The Columbia journalist James Wood Davidson had launched an attack on Simms, Hayne, and Timrod, with indiscriminate praise of the Confederate poet Harry Lyn-den Flash. Timrod's reaction was expressed in his letter to Hayne: "The dog's purpose in praising Harry so much is evident—it is indirectly to depreciate *us* who being nearer in locality to Mr. Davidson, are more in his way." [58]

George Goodwin died, and on September 6, 1864, Timrod wrote the obituary for the *Carolinian,* describing him as "this well-known merchant and citizen." Katie recovered, and on Christmas Eve gave birth to a son, Willie. Hayne quotes part of a letter that reveals Timrod's pride and delight: "At length, my dear P——, we stand upon the same height of paternity— quite a celestial elevation to me! If you could see my boy! Everybody wonders at him! He is so transparently fair; so ethereal!" [59]

X *Postwar Tragedy*

His joy was short-lived. On February 17, 1865, Columbia was sacked and burned by the Federal army. Forty years later, Julian A. Selby remembered that De Fontaine undertook to remove most of the equipment and supplies from Columbia, while "Mr. Timrod and myself remained here and issued a 'thumb-sheet' two or three times a day (not a pleasant occupa-tion, with shells dropping in the neighborhood of the building)— having retained the small amount of printing material necessary. Of course, that went up with the building." When the Federal army took over, Timrod's occupation was gone; and in addi-tion, as "one whose vigorous, patriotic editorials had made him obnoxious to Federal vengeance, Timrod was forced, while this foreign army occupied the town, to remain concealed. When they left, he rejoined his anxious 'womankind,' to behold, in common with thousands of others, such a scene of desolation as mortal eyes have seldom dwelt upon." [60]

His employment was gone, his business ruined. Timrod with his wife and son moved into Emily Goodwin's already crowded, small, one-story frame cottage. There were nine people to be fed, clothed, and kept warm: their mother, Emily and her four children, and the three in his own family. At the time, Timrod had an uncertain stipend and even more uncertain health. He attempted to find other employment, but in vain. In July he wrote to the Northern poet Richard Henry Stoddard, who had praised his volume of poems, asking if there was any chance of employment in New York City. Stoddard in an article quoted part of Timrod's letter:

I have been reduced by the destruction of this town to the most abject poverty. Literature is an unattainable and undesired luxury. I have tried to open a school, but can get no pupils, as nobody is rich enough to pay the tuition fees. All are alike ruined. . . . I have a family to support, and they must starve. With what reception would a Southerner meet in New York? Could I hope to get employment there in any capacity whatever? Hack writer of a newspaper, editor of the poet's corner of some third-rate journal, grocer's clerk—nothing would come amiss to me that would put bread into the mouths and a roof over the heads of those whom I love best in the world.

Timrod later sent some unpublished poems, but Stoddard, though he tried manfully, could neither find him a job nor place his poems. Timrod, although unjustly, was tarred as having been an ardent secessionist. [61]

In response to a request, Timrod was even more explicit in a letter to Hayne:

You ask me to tell you my story for the last year. I can embody it all in a few words—beggary, starvation, death, bitter grief, utter want of hope. But I'll be a little more particular that you may know where I stand. You know, I suppose, that the Sherman raid destroyed my business. Since that time I have been residing with my sister Mrs. Goodwin. Both my sister and myself are completely impoverished. We have lived for a long time and are still living on the gradual sale of furniture and plate. We have eaten two silver pitchers, one or two dozen forks, several sofas, innumerable chairs and a bedstead.

Most distressing was the death of his only child on October 23, 1865. In his most pathetic poem, "Our Willie," Timrod described the joy on the Christmas when he was born, and of the next "mournful Christmas by the mound/Where little Willie slept." This poem and its companion piece, "A Mother's Wail," are almost unrelieved cries of anguish and of loss.[62]

In December, De Fontaine re-established the *South Caro-linian,* but at first published it in Charleston rather than in Columbia; in February, 1866, he moved it back to Columbia. Simms and Timrod were listed as editors, but Timrod was no longer a partner in the business. Instead, he was merely "an employe," hired at fifteen dollars a week to write daily edi-torials: "I to write them in Columbia and forward them by mail. Necessity compelled me to accept the offer—I have hacked for him for four months, and have not yet received one month's pay. The truth is, Fontaine *can't* pay." The one tangible benefit from his connection with the newspaper was a railroad pass; in February, 1866, he spent three days in Charleston, and in late March he went again, to bid his friend Dr. Bruns "Good speed" before he left for London to study "pathological anatomy." The visits were not undilutedly successful; although he dined with Bruns and "went to see the lions at the circus," he came away dissatisfied: "The sum of this small experience of my native town was to this effect—that the people were as narrow-minded and selfish as ever, and that you and I and such as you and I have as much to hope at the hands of the Kamchatkans as at theirs."

This statement was not entirely just. Simms had got hold of the remaining twenty copies of Timrod's book, and peddled them at high prices to the few friends in Charleston who had money. He deliberately sent money in driblets, for he felt, as he noted later, that Timrod "suffers from the sin of impecuniosity." He also felt that his young friend submitted too readily to mis-fortune, although this lassitude was in part caused by illness. Timrod admitted freely to Hayne that he had lost hope: "I not only don't write verse now, but I feel perfectly indifferent to the fate of what I have written. I would consign ever[y] line I ever wrote to oblivion for one hundred dollars in hand. Simms had to urge me several times before I would take the trouble to send him my war lyrics." [63]

As one means of economy, the Goodwins and the Timrods moved into a house that cost $150 a year less rental. He wrote to his niece Edith on April 16, 1866, that they had been in the house about three weeks, and "like it better and better every day." Edith's mother Emily occupied the front room upstairs, "I and Katie" the back. Hopefully, he mentioned that De Fontaine was planning to re-establish the *Carolinian* in Columbia, although he would continue publishing it in Charleston, also. Timrod was to be one of the editors, and he noted that "We hope to issue the first number next Wednesday." The project languished; although Timrod continued to mention it hopefully, no issue ever appeared. [64]

Yet, as a "forlorn hope"—and, as it turned out, a vain one—he submitted poems to Northern magazines, and as recompense for writing he continued to advertise in the *Phoenix* his projected school: "Mr. Henry Timrod, with his sister, Mrs. E. T. Goodwin, proposes to open, early in October (providing a certain number of pupils can be obtained by that time) a school for girls and young ladies, at the residence of Mrs. Goodwin." [65]

When the school failed to get enough pupils to open, Timrod suggested an expedient born of desperation: that he and his wife separate, she to work as governess and he as tutor in private families. This proved unnecessary, for in November Governor James L. Orr employed him as a temporary private secretary, at a salary of one hundred dollars a month. He worked steadily for two months, until the end of the legislative session, and intermittently after that, mainly as a scribe copying or preparing official documents. By the time the regular job ended, Simms had from friends in Charleston been "fortunate enough to procure for him $115, which is eked out to him weekly at $20 per week. When that goes, God knows what the poor fellow will do, as in truth, people here are almost as destitute as himself." [66]

The New York publisher C. B. Richardson, who had just brought out Simms's *War Poetry of the South*, visited in Charleston and invited Timrod to be his guest in New York. He also talked of publishing a "richly illustrated" edition of Timrod's poems, as "the best method of introducing me to the great public"; but he seems to have wanted a guarantee in the form of an extensive subscription list. The project dragged on, but eventually came to nothing; Mrs. Goodwin, in little better health than her brother and more sceptical by nature, suspected that it was "merely a Yankee trick to get the job."

Timrod contemplated going North. His railroad pass would take him to Richmond, and for fifteen dollars he could go on to New York. If he could get to Boston, E. P. Whipple and James T. Fields, both genial fellows whom he wanted to meet, might help him to place the poems that by mail the Northern editors coldly declined, or help him to get literary work. Also, John R. Thompson had written asking for handwritten copies of some of his poems and a photograph; Thompson planned for charity to assemble a manuscript album to be raffled at a bazaar of the "Ladies of the Hollywood Memorial Association of Richmond." On March 15, 1867, Timrod sent autograph copies of "three of my poems," but apologized for not sending a photograph; he was so poor that "even the petty cost of a photograph is beyond my means." (On April 15, Timrod sent a photograph, "as a contribution of Messrs. Wearn and Hicks, Artists of Columbia, to your enterprise," and a copy of "A Mother's Wail," for Thompson's praise of it "has given me the greatest pleasure"; on May 6, a duplicate photograph.) In late March of 1867 he was forced to postpone the trip, because his wife "has had a bad hemorrhage of the lungs"; moreover, he was doubtful if he could stand the Northern climate before the middle of May.[67]

Hayne suggested that, instead, he visit at "Copse Hill," about sixteen miles from Augusta, Georgia. After the war Hayne had moved to a small farm he owned there, and lived with his mother, wife, and son in what had once been a small tenant cabin. Henry was tempted, he wrote, "not only with your light, bracing, aromatic pine-land atmosphere—the very thing I need— and with the happy prospect of your own society, but you speak of the publishers sending their *new* books! You can afford to put up with what Mr. Simms really appears to consider appetizing fare, so unctuously does he refer to it (I mean 'hog and hominy') if, mean time, instead of having your imagination starved, it (or she?) is free to wander in fresh literary pastures."

Timrod's visit that May seems to have been an unqualified success. Hayne remembered it as such:

A month's sojourn in our Robinson Crusoe solitude greatly improved both his strength and spirits. Leisure, saunterings through the great balmy pine forest, luxurious explorations of shadowy glens and valleys, full of exquisite varieties of wild flowers; the warm, dry, delicious climate which invited him to take his *dolce far niente* under the boughs of murmuring trees, outstretched upon a couch of brown pine-needles, as elastic as it was odorous, all promised to bring back his poetical enthusiasm, and to set in genial motion the half frozen springs of his invention and fancy. But his term of holiday was too limited.

Timrod feared that his undemonstrative manner, "much increased by the languor of sickness," might have made him appear insensible of the Hayne's kindness. If so, this was unintentional, for "You have ever been to me the dearest of my friends; but since my last communion with you, I have felt toward you as Jonathan to David." [68]

Timrod had been called back to Columbia partly because a "pragmatical friend, the projector of the new paper," wanted him to become the editor or chief editorial writer. Timrod accepted, at a salary of fifteen dollars a week and the hint of "willingness to give more if the paper proves a success"; but it was not to start until September, and Timrod pessimistically adds that "I look for him daily to back out of the enterprise." [69]

The improvement in health was temporary. A few weeks after returning to Columbia, he was suffering from violent headaches, and the pain in his chest "has become very acute, and my cough is almost as bad as ever." By July he had begun "to fear that the machine, my body, is slowly wearing out, and with it my mind and energies. . . . Don't think, however, that I am 'giving up.' I shall make a brave struggle for life." Under these circumstances, relatively small things offended and infuriated him. During his visit to "Copse Hill," Simms had called on the Timrod family in Columbia and had "entertained them by enlarging upon the readiness with which I yield to *mere lassitude*." Simms cited a time in Charleston when he found Timrod slightly indisposed and lying on his back reading a novel. Timrod protested indignantly: "I remember the occasion very well. I was really sick with a most painful malady—a stricture, although I didn't tell him that—and I was reading Shakespeare. I have not read ten novels in as many years, and I never read trash, not even

Mr. Simms." Even worse, Simms had impatiently refused to give Katie and Emily a chance "to say a word in my behalf." [70]

He was troubled also by the death of Sophie Sosnowski, whom he had once loved and who had remained a close friend. She had married Frank E. Schaller, a colonel in the Confederate army, and in 1865 they had moved to Athens, Georgia. There in August, 1867, she died. In his letter of condolence to Schaller, Timrod indicates that he had lost faith in immortality: after praising her beauty of character and noting that for such a loss there is "no consolation in this world," Timrod added: "You believe in the immortality of the soul, however. What an exquisite though solemn happiness it must be to you in your agony, to think that at the end of that long dark path which you will henceforth travel almost alone, a blessed Saint waits to welcome you to your rest." Mrs. Timrod was even more explicit: "A sweeter friendship than I shall ever again enjoy has been broken. . . . I am not a Christian . . . while you as a believer in our holy faith will almost catch the tones of her voice. . . . I in my earthiness can but dwell in the silence." [71]

A minor irritation was that he needed to line up contributors for the projected paper, which might be published in Charleston rather than in Columbia, but he could promise them nothing definite. The proprietor wanted to open in mid-September, Timrod wrote to Clara Dargan, but would agree only "to pay you providing his paper prove a success, and your story contribute to that success. I cannot consent to endorse such an offer to the author of 'Philip, My Son'—a tale which, in my opinion, would compare favourably with the best of Blackwood's." He had agreed to "lay the proposition before you," and to ask on what terms she would agree to write a story for the paper. [72]

His illness growing steadily worse and his chance of occupation disappearing unless he could regain a modicum of health, Timrod returned to "Copse Hill." When he wrote the *Memoir*, Hayne noted: "how sacred now, how sad and sweet are the memories of that rich, clear, prodigal August of '67!" They walked together through the woods or, reclining lazily and smoking, conversed mainly about literature. Between the visits, Timrod had indicated that Hayne had left Swinburne's "obscurity untouched"; this could be explored, and the relatively new poems of Robert Buchanan and Jean Ingelow read aloud.

Twilight was Timrod's favorite hour, and he "would often apostrophize twilight in the language of Wordsworth's sonnet." Shortly before he left, he told Hayne that he had not the slightest desire "to be an octogenarian, far less a centenarian," but that he would like to live to fifty or fifty-five. When Hayne suggested this was about Shakespeare's age, Timrod protested; he was certain that after fifty-five, "I would begin to wither, mind and body, and one hates the idea of a mummy, intellectual or physical." [73]

On September 13, ten days after he had returned to Columbia, Timrod wrote to Hayne that he had been too sick to write earlier: "You will be surprised and pained to hear that I have had a severe hemorrhage of the lungs. It came upon me without a moment's warning." Yet he had not returned "a moment too soon," for he found his family "without money or provisions. Fortunately I brought with me a small sum—I won't tell you how small—but six dollars of it was from Pollard for my last poem." The check had been delivered to him in Augusta and cashed there. He requested Hayne to acknowledge the receipt of it to Pollard, for "I use my last stamp to you." But he thought longingly of "Copse Hill": "You and Willie, your kind mother and your darling wife have made me feel as if I had two dear homes."

There is some evidence that it was about this time that Timrod stained the earlier (1862) proofsheets of his poems with blood. There seems to have been renewed talk of a collected edition, for Henry Thompson, Hugh's son, relates how "In high spirits and armed with his precious proof-sheets, he called to spend the evening with his friend Captain Hugh S. Thompson. Another caller was William H. Talley, Esq., a distinguished Columbia attorney, who had married a sister of Captain Thompson. While the three friends were conversing . . . Timrod was seized with a violent hemorrhage from the lungs, and the proof-sheets, covered with his lifeblood, fell to the floor." Timrod partially confirms this: although he does not mention the proofs, he wrote Hayne that "my mouth filled with blood while I was listening to Wm. Talley talking."

He continued to make plans. He would mail his editorials from Columbia to Charleston, but, since he would have less supervision of the paper, he was to receive only ten dollars a week. He also wrote a sonnet, almost certainly the last poem he ever wrote, "In Memoriam—Harris Simons," which he enclosed in a letter of September 16. But the letter opened by saying that "Yesterday I had another and still more copious hemorrhage. It occurred in the street—the blood came in jets from my mouth—you might have tracked me home in crimson. I am at this moment lying supine in my bed, forbidden to speak, or make any exertion whatever. But I can't resist the temptation of dropping you a line in the hope of calling forth a score or two from you in return. A letter from you would do me much good." In an undated letter written before October 1 (when Timrod was to have started work), his sister Emily wrote: "Yesterday I had to write and for him renounce the office. Does it not seem strange that just when we had some prospect of at least a pittance, the hope should be withdrawn." [74]

Until the twentieth of September he was in critical condition, but before the twenty-fifth he had rallied sufficiently for Emily to write Hayne that he was much better. Friends helped as best they could. A friend in Charleston sent fifteen dollars, Hayne sent ten, and little Willie Hayne a gold dollar. Friends like Thompson and General Wade Hampton helped, and Doctors R. W. Gibbes and A. N. Talley offered him free medical services and "spent hours by his bedside, endeavoring by every human means to arrest the progress of the disease; but pneumonic symptoms made their appearance, and hope was gone!"

According to Emily, in these last days the "idea that he was to *choke* to death by a sudden rush of blood from the lungs, haunted him like a spectre." This did not happen, but on October 2nd he suffered another hemorrhage, and on the 4th Dr. Gibbes told him that "I can see no chance of your recovery." Startled, he looked up and said: "And is *this* to be the end of all—so soon! so soon! and I have achieved so little! I thought to have done so much! I had just before my first attack fallen into a strain of such pure and delicate fancies. I do think this winter I would have done more than I have ever done; yes, I should have written more purely, and with a greater delicacy. And then I have loved you all so much."

During this last illness, he had turned back for consolation to religion, keeping a New Testament near his pillow and "now and then" asking Emily to read him "a chapter from the Gospels, and to pray with him." On Sunday, October 6, he received Holy Communion from an Episcopal clergyman. Yet he tried, also, to will himself to live. After a series of strong convulsions that for hours "shook his already worn-out frame," Emily murmured that he would soon be at at rest, but Timrod mournfully replied, "Yes, my sister, *but love is sweeter than rest!*" At five Monday morning, Katie took Emily's place. When she attempted to give him water, he could not swallow. His last words were: "Never mind. I shall soon drink of the river of eternal life." He died at full daybreak on October 7, 1867. His body was buried beside that of his son in the Trinity Church cemetery, in Columbia.[75]

CHAPTER 2

Poet of Love and Nature

I *Young Poet*

THE EARLIEST KNOWN POETRY of Henry Timrod is preserved in a stained and faded manuscript, entitled "Autographic Relics" and now lavishly bound, in the Charleston Library Society. All of these poems have been carefully transcribed, edited, and printed in Guy Cardwell's *The Uncollected Poems of Henry Timrod*. Where later printed versions are recorded, these have been checked and collated with the manuscript, and significant variants have been indicated. A preliminary statement by William A. Courtenay has it that Timrod gave the pages, in a brown paper cover, to Ursula Strohecker, later Mrs. Ursula S. Bird, and that "through many changes and vicissitudes, of war and peace, these manuscript pages had been carefully preserved: of course crumpled, soiled, and in bad condition." Mrs. Bird is not quite so precise; she wrote in 1896 that the scrapbook and a copy of William Henry Timrod's "To Harry," "were given me by Mr. Eugene B. Baker—my cousin by marriage, and Henry Timrod's *close friend,* and admirer." The thirty-five sheets contain seventy-nine poems, some incomplete; Courtenay had the pages cleaned as well as he could before he had the sheets bound.[1]

The earliest date given is 1843, when Timrod would have been fourteen or fifteen years old. A note says the poem was "Written in a blank leaf of Thompson's [*sic*] Castle of Indolence," and beside the poem is the name "Ursula." It is deliberately archaic. Thomson had created a fancied realm; Timrod wrote,

Where pleasure cheaply bought beguil'd the hour
    And lazy wight withouten boisterous glee

Might easy live, ne die of ennui
But in our Carolinian atmosphere
We feel thy force in sad reality,
And all thy ills without thy pleasures rare
Weigh us poor mortals down, cooped in the school room here.
(Cardwell, 78)

More appealing, and certainly much more closely in the school-boy tradition, is the rollicking parody of Charles Wolfe's poem celebrating the death (probably imaginary) of an unpopular tutor.

Most of these poems, whether written in Charleston or in Athens, seem to belong to his college days. Many of them are definitely imitative. In seeking to master a technique, Timrod used as models not only the poems of Wordsworth, Shelley, Byron, and Moore, and a bit later Tennyson and Browning; he also turned back to Catullus, Anacreon, and the Greek Anthology. Some of his epigrams, especially, have a sharpness, if not a polish, that reminds one of the lesser Greek poets. Typical of this work is his

Apology to Tom for Maltreating his 'Friend'

If it be true as I have often heard,
(And this has prov'd its author has not err'd)
That "fellow feeling makes us wondrous kind,"
We could not wonder that thy heart inclin'd
To aid thy hapless pet and kindred brute.
But Tom forgive us that we scorn'd thy suit,
Hogs may be very pleasant company
But we had one already Tom in thee.
(Cardwell, 52)

Most of the identifiable college poems, however, were love poems. Hayne noted that "Some of the cleverest of these love-songs were published" over a fictitious signature in the Charleston *Evening News*. Only two of these have been identified; in these instances, Timrod's disguise consisted simply of reversing his initials. The first is a sonnet dealing with man's desire "to tear aside the veil,/That kindly overshades Futurity," and his own personal intent to "steer with fearless soul/Tho' storms divide me from the long'd for goal." It is a youthful poem, but it was meant to be philosophical, even though it hardly deserves that appellation; and it continues to show the young Timrod's infatuation with what he considered poetic devices, such as needless apostrophes. The second poem may be described as ironically amatory. Cupid may prefer to lurk in a soft blue eye, although some lovers prefer sterner dark eyes, or gray, or brown, or hazel. The poet's favorite is the one that, regardless of color, smiles sweetly on him; but he is no slave: "When it frowns, I break the spell/Another'll suit me quite as well." [2]

In "Autographic Relics" there are several other poems to or about Cupid. Most of them are incomplete; they are light and fanciful, with an occasional use of a mild conceit; and they tend to play upon words. Thus, if a certain young lady keeps his heart in jail, she must "as pledge to keep it *whole*/Give me hers prisoner *on parole*" (Cardwell, 58).

Many of the love poems were addressed directly to young ladies. A few of these, like Anne Waddel of Athens and Mrs. Arabella Anna Caskin, are readily identifiable; there seems little likelihood of attempted disguise in names like Mary or Marie or Cousin Lou; but a pastoral name like Chloe or a quaint one like Florabel may easily be getting over into the realm of imaginary or idealized persons. In nearly all of the poems the poet seems to be going through the motions of making love, of preparing gracefully versified tributes to stimulating young beauties, rather than expressions of personal love or of passion or of even deep emotion. No doubt, as he wrote Hayne, a pretty girl's face acted upon him like an inspiration. But contemporary friends like Hayne and Bruns, and later critics like Ludwig Lewisohn and Jay B. Hubbell, have emphasized Timrod's rigorous apprentice work in training his poetic talent. These early lyrics in a variety of forms and meters may have seemed a fit method of disciplining his poetic emotions.[3]

II *Poet of Nature*

More important are his poems about nature. Hayne has noted that in those days "Timrod looked up to Wordsworth as his poetical guide and exemplar," and Hayne remembered him "in his early manhood repeating in a deep, musical bass voice, his favorite 'ode' on 'Intimations of Immortality from Recollections of early Childhood.' . . . it was impossible to listen to him with-

out catching some spark of his fiery enthusiasm." Nature possessed a healing power, as Timrod indicated in such poems as
"The Breezes Through the Woodlands Moan" and "In the Deep
Shadow." [4] In them too the essentially melancholy strain in his
nature becomes evident. But the best of the nature poems were
written some years later.

The first major encouragement that Timrod and Hayne
received was not from Charleston editors, but from Virginian
John R. Thompson, editor of the *Southern Literary Messenger*.
As early as January, 1849, Timrod contributed a double sonnet
on Arabella that was widely reprinted in newspapers; in the next
decade he continued to contribute frequently to that magazine.
Until February, 1856, he signed these poems with the pseudonym "Aglaus," the name of a Greek pastoral poet; in that
issue his "Lines" are signed Henry Timrod, and the editor
identified him as Aglaus. But there was also personal encouragement and stimulus. Hayne remembered it vividly in a letter to
Margaret Junkin Preston: "In the spring of '49 (I being then a
mere lad at College) and Timrod a Law-Student in Petigru's
office, Thompson visited Charleston. . . . How vividly I recall his
appearance! Just 26 years old, slightly, but elegantly formed,
with a manner far quicker and more vivacious, than it was in
after life,—dressed in the height of the prevailing mode, with
light-twilled pantaloons, and a blue coat, brass-buttoned,—he
shone upon us 'Hobbledhoys'—a somewhat radiant vision of a
man partly *litterateur,* and partly dandy! We liked him none
the less, however. . . ." Since the editor was equally enthusiastic
about them and anxious to print their poems, it is not remark-
able that the young Charlestonians remembered him with "a
peculiar tenderness." [5]

Timrod's most popular contribution was a didactic poem, "The
Past." It was "so full of subdued thoughtfulness and beauty, that
after having been republished by scores of periodicals, it came
under the notice of a distinguished Northern gentleman, himself
an author [Whittier], who, corresponding with a friend in
Charleston, expressed his hearty admiration of the lines. . . .
The letter was shown to Timrod, and its encouraging effect was
greater and more permanent, than could be understood by any
person not gifted in some degree with the susceptibility of
genius." The poem deserved its popularity. It is not over-

weighted with didacticism; it is simple and clean-cut; and the excellent conclusion pictures the present being absorbed into the past, yet no more dying than the spirit dies.[6]

One of the longest and most characteristic of his nature poems, "The Summer Bower," was published in the *Southern Literary Messenger* in August, 1852. The poet had often gone into this grove; he describes it lovingly, for always there, when depressed by grief or disturbed by joy, he had "found the calm I looked for, or returned/Strong with the quiet rapture in my soul." But one July day he went there, discontented and sick in mind without any real cause, and found for once "No medicinal virtue." Nature can comfort grief and in her own way sympathize with human suffering, but she offers no consolation for the vain repinings or sickly sentiments "Engendered of weak, unquiet heart." For these nature has no solace, but rebukes them with contempt (*Poems*, 106-8).

Although he was writing and publishing with fair regularity, Timrod was discontented with his accomplishment. Part of this discontent was no doubt caused by his dislike of teaching and tutoring, by the simple necessity of earning a living; but part of it, assuredly, was caused by his inability to fix in print his poetic ideas and ideals. Too often he was "haunted all night" and all day by "the ghost of a song, by the shade of a lay." In fact, frequently the fancy which had seemed so charming in his mind while it remained one of his "butterfly-dreams" would die into prosaicness "with the fleeting lay/Into which it is wrought." Too often one feels desire beneath the lines, not conviction; dreams, not philosophy or reflection. Yet he suffered much from his inability to loose the feelings that stirred within him (*Poems*, 31, 45).

III *Youthful Critic*

He thought much about poets and poetry. An early sonnet rather youthfully advised the poet bent on "lasting fame" to look to his own heart and home, to the earth as he knows it, and to remain humble. The poet then may "draw from matters of the hearth/Truths wide as nations, and as deep as love" (*Poems*, 170). A far more ambitious attempt to put his ideas on poetry into words is in his longest poem. True, a protecting cloak of fiction and of poetic convention is thrown around the attempt; the protagonist is an anonymous fictional character. But the sentiments spoken by him and to him are the beliefs of Henry Timrod; in thought, although not in fact, the work is auto-biographical.

"A Vision of Poesy" is the product of youth; it is, Hayne notes, marred "by a too evident lack of harmony and unity of parts, proceeding from the fact that the narrative was composed in sections, and after the lapse of periods so long between the different *bouts* of composition, that much of the original fervor of both conception and execution must have evaporated." The underlying concept is clear enough. Timrod is presenting the subjective sources of poetry; or, in Hayne's phrase, "the true laws which underlie and determine the noblest uses of the poetical faculty."

The protagonist as a youth had more than ordinary sensibility. Strange portents had marked his birth; afterward, the child had seemed withdrawn; he frightened his parents by a strange far look and by "brief snatches of mysterious rhymes." He is conscious of uncomprehended mysteries, of an intuitive understanding which he can not order with thought, and of strange emanations from natural phenomena. He is troubled by dreams and disturbed by thoughts that alike elude his grasp. One night when he had gone in solitude to a favorite nook deep in the woods, a spirit appears to him—or seems to appear. She is the angel of Poesy, and she reveals the high mission of the true poet.

The task of Poesy is closely related to that of religion, though definitely subordinate to this "mightier Power." She helps to keep the world spiritually "forever fresh and young"; to arouse in men the nobler emotions and desires; to "turn life's tasteless waters into wine"; and to inspire poets to seek as much knowledge as men can learn and then to translate it so that ordinary men can understand it. But Poesy can only "sow the germ which buds in human art." The poet himself determines the result. If, as poet, he is worthy, he must be pure and consecrated; he must belong "to the whole wide world." Timrod deliberately reverses the famous statement of Keats on beauty and truth: the poet must be "assured that Truth alone/Is Beauty." Mindful of this, he sings not merely for himself or of his own subjective thoughts and longings; he sings for those who grope and wonder, and can not sing.

Timrod breaks off the fable to comment directly on the inability of the poet to present his full concept. The idea had seemed alive "to the Poet's hope within my heart," but as it became an actuality, the concept lost its semblance of life.

The third section of "A Vision of Poesy" describes a man grown old while yet in the prime of life, a poet who has largely failed because, misunderstanding the sources of art, he has yielded to a morbid subjectivity. This concern with self, partly brought on by the scorn of the world and by the disdain of the woman he loved, had vitiated his poetic accomplishment. He returns home to die. But the angel of Poesy appears to console him. Although the fault of hidden selfishness had marred his verse, he had been scornful of specious falsehood, and he had uttered "Truths that for man might else have slumbered long." This ingrown morbidity had prevented his attaining full stature, for the great poet "spheres worlds in himself." He must be concerned with the mysteries of his own soul and mind, but "on the surface of his song these lie/As shadows, not as darkness": he makes use of the personal light to help clarify the general darkness. Timrod points the contrast between partial achievement and completeness. A complete poem is an ethical poem; it not only functions within itself, it acts upon the world to make for positive good. His terms are romantic, and his words often abstract.

As a poem, "A Vision of Poesy" is uneven, frequently unconvincing, and at best achieves only a limited success; as a vehicle for his critical theories, it is less persuasive than his essay, "A Theory of Poetry." Several writers have suggested that Timrod in this poem was greatly influenced by Shelley's "Alastor." Since Timrod's immature work seems a beginning yet also an integral part of his critical theory, it is useful to compare the two poems.

Both Shelley and Timrod wrote of an idealistic young poet who finds tragedy rather than a fulfillment of genius; in each poem, the young man broods in solitude upon the majesty and the mystery of nature. The resemblances are circumstantial, not spiritual. Alastor is essentially Shelleyan, or Byronic. He is dedicated to poetry, to earth, to nature. But in his quest of the spirit of poetry he left an "alienated home,/To seek strange truths in undiscovered lands"; he has pursued "Nature's most secret steps" in strange and far-off places and in the "awful ruins of the days of old." It is essentially a traveler's concept of nature, not a mystic's; the revelation that he could never hope to find at home might somehow come to him in Arabia or Ethiopia or the Arctic. Although Shelley states the opposite, Alastor apparently seeks understanding through experience and not through contemplation. Timrod's young poet has an entirely different concept of nature. He is more Wordsworthian than Shelleyan, but he lacks Wordsworth's certitude and spiritual rapport with nature. It is the Wordsworthian mystical comprehension that he seeks. For that, he goes deep into the woods and takes as teachers the leaves, the trees, the stars, the sky, and the wind. He depends upon intuitive reverie, rapt contemplation, and revelation; he seeks them in the familiar solitude of his own region instead of in the wanderings of Alastor.

Each poem uses a dream symbol. But Alastor's is a simple dream of a maid who typifies the spirit of poesy. Her voice "was like the voice of his own soul." She represents the unattainable perfection that he yearned for. She is an oriental goddess or houri for whom Alastor feels a physical as well as mental passion; having known her in a dream, he can never be satisfied with the earthly love that a woman can give. His wanderings become wilder, more frantic: seemingly, the ideal unattainable in life might somehow be attained in death. The anonymous poet in "A Vision of Poesy" does not have the sensation of "shuddering limbs and . . . gasping breath"; he is not, in fact, quite certain whether he has in his solitude dreamed of a maiden, or been visited by a spirit: " 'Here was it that I saw, or dreamed I saw,/I know not which, that shape of love and light.' "

However briefly, Alastor possessed the maid who personified poetry; in Timrod's vision, Poesy remains aloof and remote. She will not give the young poet full knowledge of the mysteries, but only so much as a mortal can know. Even then, she limits her promise severely. She gives the fire and genius, but the "true bard is his own only Fate." The poet fails in Timrod's version through his own human faults and not through a vain quest after the unattainable. He too has known solitude, brought on him by the scorn of a material world and that of a beautiful woman.

But Poesy, while she comforts him, places the blame directly on him; he has grown too enwrapped in his own thoughts, and he has heeded too little the cares and aspirations of other people.

Timrod's concept of the ideal has little relation to Shelley's. Alastor sought a perfection that had, except in the strikingly physical personification of poesy as a woman, no concern with the things or people of this world; he sought it by romantic, concretely geographical wanderings. In his Preface, Shelley notes that "The Poet's self-centred seclusion was avenged by the furies of an irresistible passion pursuing him to speedy ruin." But Alastor is self-centered before his dream, as well as afterward; and the dream itself encourages this egoism and leads him to destruction. Timrod's poet fails, at least in part, because he forgets or ignores the nobility of his vision. He has had his moments of insight and of accomplishment. He has been "A priest, and not a victim at the shrine." His work has had positive value; it leads to loneliness and sorrow, but not to ruin.

In death, as in life, these imaginary poets present basic differences that are more important than their superficial resemblances. Shelley set out to write an allegorical tragedy; Timrod sought to give meaning to a poet's life through a complex vision. Even the machinery and the forms of the poems differ. Timrod may have found in "Alastor" a suggestion that kindled his poetic imagination; but Timrod's philosophy was too far removed from Shelley's for this suggestion to do more than start him on his own way.

In other respects, Timrod's resemblance to Shelley is slight. Each believed in the nobility and the mystical power of poetry; each man was integrally a part of the Romantic Movement. Timrod had read Shelley's "A Defence of Poetry," and twice he quotes approvingly, but inaccurately, the definition of poetry as "the record of the best and happiest moments of the happiest and best minds." These words had impressed Timrod as truth; he was in full agreement. But the extent of his disagreement with Shelley's ideas is most apparent in their respective treatment of inspiration. In the paragraph preceding his definition, Shelley had identified poetry as something divine, and the poem as supernally inspired: "I appeal to the greatest poets of the present day, whether it is not an error to assert that the finest passages of poetry are produced by labour and study. The toil and the delay recommended by critics can be justly interpreted to mean no more than a careful observation of the inspired moments, and an artificial connexion of the spaces between their suggestions by the intertexture of conventional expressions."

Without mentioning Shelley's words and probably without considering them worth a rejoinder, Timrod contradicts this theory of art. He insists on making a clean and sharp distinction between the subjective essence of poetry and the objective, tangible poem. This distinction governs his treatment of inspiration. He felt that a poet's mind had to be stimulated, roused, inspired. The stimulation might come from within, through a chance daydream or dazzling thought; it might come after long contemplation of some natural or human phenomenon; the spark might be kindled by some external pretty face or casual word. But this inspiration, whatever its cause, acted upon the mind of the poet, taking hold of his imagination or being played upon by his fancy. There was a mystical quality involved; the poet differed from the ordinary man principally in his being able to express this inspiration: "The ground of the poetic character is more than ordinary sensibility."

When he presented his idea of inspiration through the objectifying medium of poetry, Timrod emphasized the mystical concept. His youthful poet not only gets a sense of mystery from the trees, skies, and winds, but also murmurs rhymes which he does not himself understand, and feels dull, clinging memories of a mystic tongue and of a once-clear comprehension. Inspiration, embodied in the form of the angel of Poesy, rouses, troubles, and perplexes his soul; and it drives his mind on to such knowledge as mortals can attain; she is the light of the poetic imagination. Yet even in this romantic concept, Timrod allows to inspiration only the function of beginning the poetic process. The poet's reach depends upon himself. He alone can govern his poem, and he must do it through his own knowledge and technique.[7]

"A Vision of Poesy" was too long and perhaps too uneven for magazine publication. In the meantime, Timrod had found another outlet for his verse. In May, 1852, Hayne became assistant editor of the *Southern Literary Gazette,* published in Charleston; within a year, he became editor and owner, as the only possible way of getting eight hundred dollars that was owed to him for contributions and for editorial work. He was delighted to publish Timrod's new poems, and he also republished, with slight revision, several that had already appeared in the *Southern Literary Messenger.*

The most interesting of the new poems is called "Dramatic Fragment" (*Poems,* 105-6). The title may indicate that Timrod had started a play, and was salvaging one part that seemed reasonably complete. It is a dramatic monologue on the wrongness of trying to shape a boy in a commonplace mold that will make him a replica of his elders. The brother and father to whom the speech is addressed has forgotten that the boy has "A soul as different and distinct from thine/As love of goodness is from love of glory/Or noble poesy from noble prose." Men are born, Timrod thinks, "in miniature completeness/And like each other only in our weakness." This is an excellent example of Timrod's plea for the right to individuality, in education and in life.[8]

The *Southern Literary Gazette* soon folded, but Timrod continued to publish intermittently in the *Southern Literary Messenger,* the *Charleston College Magazine,* and other regional periodicals. But he was keenly aware that his poems had not received national recognition and that he had no chance of making a living from his poetry. Apparently his writing became more desultory and spasmodic, and in truth less interesting to us, until the establishment of *Russell's Magazine* gave him a secure outlet and spurred him to new efforts.

IV *Russell's Magazine*

The magazine was planned in John Russell's bookshop by a group of Charleston scholars and literary men. Its editor, for the three years and six volumes of its existence, was Paul Hamilton Hayne; the initial number appeared on what the editor later called an "ominous date," April 1, 1857. It could pay little even for serialized novels; it paid to most contributors, including Timrod, nothing. Timrod seems to have had no hand in the editorial policy or work, but he contributed to almost every issue.

"The Arctic Voyager" appeared in the first number. In it, Hayne wrote, "we detect for the first time in our author's art, the influence of Tennyson, not superseding, but harmoniously blending with the earlier influence of Wordsworth." Timrod freely acknowledges a general indebtedness, and implies that it began earlier than Hayne realized: "I yield to few, and only to that extravagant few who would put him over the head of Milton himself, in my admiration of Poe, and I yield to none in a love which is almost a worship of Tennyson, with whose poems I have been familiar from boyhood, and whom I yet continue to study with ceaseless profit and pleasure. But I can by no means consent to regard him as the first of Poets." [9]

The indebtedness to Tennyson's "Ulysses" is obvious and striking. Timrod may have intended deliberately to suggest a modern parallel with an ancient legend. This would explain his borrowing both in structure and in thought. The early part has the tone of a soliloquy, but the last twelve lines are addressed directly to "my hardy shipmates." Throughout, the narrator is Captain Elisha Kent Kane, the Arctic explorer. Twice he has tried to reach the Pole, once by land and once by sea; twice he has been baffled, but not daunted. He may fail again, but he will not count the chances; even if he perishes, it will not be in vain, for "never in this life/Is labor wholly fruitless," or a lofty hope entirely unrewarded. [10]

V Poetic Devices

Timrod continued to experiment with poems to or about women. In one of these, "A Year's Courtship," he depicts himself as the listener to whom a friend narrates the progress of his courtship from first seeing the girl, through the troubled and uncertain days when she was coy and undecided, and on to the period of acceptance, happiness, and approaching marriage. The quatrains are simple, yet expertly handled; the rhymes (lines one and three, two and four) are easy and unforced. [11]

An entirely different type of poem brought what seems to have been his first appearance in a magazine with nationwide circulation, *Harper's*. "Three Pictures" describes in fairly regular blank verse three vividly contrasting girls in a painting; they are half-draped, and stand by the edge of a stream. The first is a brunette, dark-eyed, voluptuous, passionate; she is the ideal of South European beauty. The second is blond, cool and unawakened, yet craving to be loved; she reminds one of Freya in her classic northern beauty. The third is from the East, with Oriental (presumably Jewish) grace and with a beauty "Brown-skinned and glossy as a Spanish nut." The three girls are described separately, objectively, and at length; then they move the poet to sing of them, for he realizes that, while contrasting, their beauties mingle into harmony, into

> One glorious chord of beauty, on my soul
> Striking divinest unison! For thus
> Hath God ordained it; to the poet's eye
> All beauty is alike, and ye, I swear,
> Are beautiful as eve and noon and dawn
> Shining together on the wondering earth!
> (Cardwell, 86-91)

He followed this work with a poem light and playful in tone, with a deliberate imitation or echoes of Browning's mannerisms of rhyme and of far-fetched allusions. "Præceptor Amat" is in rhyming couplets, and is a soliloquy by a tutor about the attractive young lady (actually, Felicia Robinson) whom he is trying, amid numerous distractions, to teach Greek. That morning she brings him flowers and, usurping his office, instructs him in the knowledge and lore of flowers; if he does not thank her "in a sweet English rhyme . . . She'd be—oh! she'd be—a real Saracen Omar/To a certain much-valued edition of Homer." Timrod works in a Greek rhyme, and he describes various flowers, including one that he secretes in his bosom. He implies that the apparently "stern, passionless Tutor" is infatuated with the girl; but at the end he rouses from dreaming, disregards the flowers, and commands, "here is your book!" It is one of Timrod's pleasantest, most graceful works (*Poems,* 12-16).

"The Lily Confidante" marks his first successful use of a poetic device that he was to sharpen and to use far more effectively in some later poems, especially "Charleston" and "Spring": personification. According to one's taste, personification may be considered a minor myth or a pathetic fallacy, or both. In any case, Timrod confides in the garden lily his love for a young lady whose name is also Lily; other flowers attempt to eavesdrop, and may reveal his secret. He then asks the lily for advice, for "I am puzzled how to woo"; rather lengthily, the lily advises him to be simple and direct in his plea, for "Love's the lover's only magic,/Truth the very subtlest art." [12]

The one other poem to be considered in this group developed out of what Timrod considered to be authentic love. Even so, it seems more a tribute than a song of passion. He was in love with Sophie Sosnowski and proposed to her at least once, although his love cooled markedly after Sophie made fun of his passion and advised him to "be a man." Before that, however, she had warned him that she intended to remain unmarried and had asked that he paint her "future as a maid." In "Two Portraits," Timrod complied, but he went beyond her original request. He imagined her at forty, still beautiful, friendly, beloved by family and friends, yet conscious of some incompleteness in her life. This was what "Might, but will never be your lot." In the second and contrasting section, he imagines Sophie at the same age, but as a wife and mother. Now she has attained true beauty and completeness. The poet cannot divine the name of her husband or her place of residence or even whether she is rich or poor; but he has never seen "a form or face/To which more plainly have been lent/The blessing of a full content." But if Timrod convinced himself in this skillfully done poem that "the wife's lovelier than the maid," he did not convince Sophie—at least in his own right. [13]

There was no significant change in Timrod's attitude toward nature, only an intensification of his regret that he could not find in it the same strength that Wordsworth had found. The cause was in himself: "I myself would be a far happier man if I could follow his teaching, rather than my own dark and perturbed spirit." Typically, he describes how, being vexed by a book in which he had deliberately sought a "plausible likeness of my own dark thoughts," he had gone into the woods in which he had often found peace. That day nature did not help him. He remained passively languorous, without energy to move or think, until a little child restored to him faith and life. [14] This poignant inability, this longing, was expressed memorably in one of his finest sonnets:

> At last, beloved Nature! I have met
> Thee face to face upon thy breezy hills,
> And boldly, where thy inmost bowers are set,
> Gazed on thee naked in thy mountain rills.

When first I felt thy breath upon my brow,
Tears of strange ecstasy gushed out like rain,
And with a longing, passionate as vain,
I strove to clasp thee. But, I know not how,
Always before me didst thou seem to glide;
And often from one sunny mountain-side,
Upon the next bright peak I saw thee kneel,
And heard thy voice upon the billowy blast;
But, climbing, only reached that shrine to feel
The shadow of a Presence which had passed.

(Poems, 176)

A third significant concept, that of intuitive reverie and of dreams, strengthened his poetry of the 1850's. Since Timrod was not by temperament a philosopher, his approach to an understanding of life was through intuition rather than reason. He caught illuminating and sometimes puzzling glimpses into unfathomed mysteries; he was convinced that these glimpses were authentic, though he was not able to his own satisfaction to define what they were. As a result, he set a high value on intuitive reverie and on meditative contemplation. If he could not actively and forcibly wrench a concept of truth from the universe, he might by a willing passivity achieve some understanding of truth. This represented a road to comprehension but not to expression. These mystical concepts were to him the subjective essence of which poetry is made, but the essence must be given objective form by ordered thought and by artistry. The illuminating core of meaning was not capable of being made explicit by a blunt, direct statement: the explanation must be indirect, and it must be conceived within the conventions of poetry.

For this artistic purpose Timrod uses frequently the concept and the device of the dream. The significance of his usage varies. To him the word "dream" had rich and varied connotations; he liked its sound, its meaning, and its overtones; he used dreams to suggest a pleasant, airy fancy, a quality of withdrawal, a flash of understanding, and a physical or mental fact. The symbol works directly, on an elementary level. Timrod made very little distinction between the daydream and the sleep-dream. Both were products of the subconscious. Although he shied away from definition, Timrod apparently thought of the daydream as a creative process and of the sleep-dream as an uncontrolled revelation. In either case the dream is not separated from the real by any sharp line of demarcation. It is an extension of reality rather than escape from it. In two poems, once speaking in his own right and once through a protagonist, Timrod wrote, "I saw, or dreamed I saw." This confusion of the senses was deliberate. Whether experienced during waking or sleeping hours, the dream cuts through the surface appearances to an inner or to a supernal reality.

Thus the dream becomes a means of knowing one's self. As conscious beings, we are physically and to a large degree mentally bound to matter, space, and time; we are cut off from any effective communion or communication with the spiritual. The contrast Timrod sought to make was between matter-of-factness and ideality, or between materialism and spirituality; for to his mind ideality and reality were not opposites: they appear at times to be so only because men fail to understand their basic kinship. Timrod stated the power of the intuitive reverie most clearly in his poem "Dreams" (1857). He begins with a denial that dreams are false; on the contrary, the shadowy thoughts that pass unnoticed or suffer stern repression in the daylight come out at night like the stars. Whether good or evil, these night visitors are "allegories with their roots in truth,/ That tell us solemn secrets of ourselves."

In this poem, man's hope was first of all a vision. It could not be proved by scientific or philosophical knowledge; such proof as there was must be reached through intuitive reverie and through revelation. Here the dream took on a new power. Through it the mind dredged up dim wishes and records long erased from the consciousness; it caught foreshadowings of a misty future. But this poem did not satisfy Timrod as expressing his belief, or else he felt he had not sufficiently exorcised the ghosts from the unknown: in *Poems* (1859) he published a thoroughly revised version of what is essentially the same poem. The revisions accentuate man's helplessness in a land of mystery; they emphasize more sharply the essential allegorical truth. In the second version Timrod seems more concerned than before with a third use of the dream: as a means of understanding ultimate truth. Self-understanding continues to bulk large in the poem, but it becomes linked more surely with a knowledge that goes beyond self.

Timrod was intensely conscious of a need for linking the personal and the universal. Along with this, he possessed a sense of identification with the past so troublesome that in one sonnet he asked if his wild thoughts were indeed the product of his heart and brain, or if he had somewhere, sometime shared martyrdoms and deep griefs and mighty pleasures. He sought the answer in the immediacy of reverie. In this sonnet, where he is expressing his thought subjectively, Timrod's confusion of the dream and of the reality may represent only an attempt to reveal his own state of mind.

In "A Vision of Poesy," Timrod had used the same device, though less effectively. This spiritual biography of an imaginary poet is an embodiment of Timrod's creed. It helps to clarify his concept of dream and revelation. The protagonist is pictured in his youth as given to a kind of creative daydreaming, which brought him closer to a perception of nature than any observation could have achieved. This Wordsworthian feeling about nature was supplemented by mystifying dreams of identification with supernal powers that spoke to him in a mysterious language. Poesy is at once a vision and an actuality; as "the angel of the earth" she appears to the poet in the guise of a maiden; but poesy remains also a subjective essence. The imaginary poet sees the maiden and hears her voice: he gains from her the conviction that a poet must be a part of ordinary, everyday life, yet at the same time he must be capable of understanding the mysteries behind that life. Here as elsewhere Timrod makes clear his belief that only the germ of understanding can be won through the vision or reverie; the development must grow through knowledge and experience; its expression can be achieved only by personal artistry.

Without the germ or essence, however, there can be no poetry worth writing or worth talking about. Significantly, the imaginary poet does not know whether he saw and heard Poesy or whether she is only the product of his own subconscious aspirations. His vision is a symbol of the ideal. Whether the angel appeared or not is immaterial. What does matter to Timrod and to his poet is that by means of the vision a man can find a spiritual faith for himself. Through the dream symbol Timrod adumbrates his own conception of the poet's function, which is closely related to that of the priest. He belongs to the world, not to himself; he is a minister of truth, not of personal feeling; his use of a subjective incandescence must be to help clarify the general darkness.

Timrod's poet failed, as Timrod himself often felt that he had failed, because he yielded to the Janus-faced evils of materialism and of subjectivity. For the dream, as Timrod conceived it, was not complete as a thing within itself. It was a token of the ideal. But true reality and the ideal, if one could fully comprehend them, would turn out to be identical. The vision is an allegory of life, and it is life.

The dream concept served Timrod as an ethical basis, but he did not find it fully satisfying as a base on which to ground his poetry. He could accept the reality of the dream, but his poems indicate that he was uncertain of its ultimate truth. Reverie, interpreted by the poet as he will, remains personal. To secure a catharsis by expressing a personal belief there must be complete conviction in the idea and full satisfaction with the mode of expression. In Timrod's case, reverie seemed complete within itself, and therefore satisfying until he attempted to objectify it, but too often at that point his brain was bewildered "with a cunning and specious appearance of thought/I seem to be catching but never have caught." [15]

But the concept of dreams, like those of nature and of love, did not give Timrod the full poetic and intellectual release that he desired. Part of his dissatisfaction was, simply, with the finished product—with his failure as an artist. But it was also, in part, a discontent aroused by the realization that so many of his thoughts were unutterable because they were incomplete.

His friends thought better of his work than he did. In 1859 he collected and to some extent revised what he considered the best of his early work. According to Simms, this "volume of his poems was published (nominally) by Ticknor and Fields, of Boston. This was published at the request of friends, and by the aid of friends. The publishers did nothing for the work, as they rarely will do where they are not themselves the proprietors." Bruns states, also, that the book was published by subscription.

The book received comparatively little attention. Timrod's friends blamed this, with some justice, on the troubled times and on partisan feeling. Hayne's caustic remark is that "some even of the critics of the North did not hesitate to commend it," and he quotes with approval from a review in the New York *Tribune:* "These poems are worthy of a wide audience. They form a welcome offering to the common literature of our country. The author, whose name promises to be better known from this specimen of his powers, betrays a genuine poetic instinct in the selection of his themes, and has treated them with a lively, delicate fancy, and a graceful beauty of expression." A reviewer in *Harper's,* also, was favorably impressed, and he noted that "Mr. Timrod's name now comes before us for the first time, but he has given assurance in this volume that he will not remain a stranger in the walks of American poetry." These were isolated cases. All of Timrod's literary friends have, with variation only in the wording, agreed with Bruns that the book "fell almost dead from the press." [16]

Yet even his closest friends had some reservations. Simms and Bruns use exactly the same word in describing Timrod's muse as "reticent." Timrod did not write easily. To Simms, this was a serious defect, traceable in part to lack of will and of effort; to Bruns, it was worthy of praise that he "never lisped in numbers from any mere impulse of utterance." They also recognized that many poems showed promise rather than ultimate achievement. The prejudiced Hayne, after proclaiming that a "better first volume of the kind has seldom appeared anywhere," admitted that some of the poems were uneven and lacked harmony. They agreed also that Timrod's works were meditative rather than philosophical or passionate. But he was not basically a descriptive poet. He was "not so much concerned with the passing phenomenon as with the permanent truth it suggested." [17]

Literary historians and critics have largely disregarded these contemporary verdicts. When he is known at all, Timrod is mainly known as a war poet, and as one characterized by the restricting and unfair phrase, "Laureate of the Confederacy." In one sense this is fair enough: his later poetry is definitely better poetry. But, rightly, he did not regard himself as a war poet. At the beginning of the Civil War, he was partisan; but his best poems deal with the horror of war, regardless of which side is victor or victim. These poems grew out of his earlier work. Some, like "Spring" and "Christmas," are rounded and complete; but so are some of the earlier poems. By 1859, Timrod was well out of his apprenticeship. These early poems deserve more attention than they have received, as authentic poetry in their own right. It is also true, however, that he could not have written the later poems if as a young man he had not achieved a partial unriddling of the mysteries of life through the concepts of nature, love, and dreams.

CHAPTER 3

Ethical Critic

I *Criticism in Poems*

SEVERAL of Timrod's poems might with propriety be considered as part of his literary criticism. This is especially true of "A Vision of Poesy," which shows his preoccupation with the ethical aspects of poetry and with the poet's obligation to translate for the mass-mind the aspirations and thoughts which, otherwise, it could never grasp. He was also concerned because the values of the world seemed to be material values; those of poetry were spiritual, ethical, aesthetic. He could find no way to reconcile these opposites. Yet if poetry was to have meaning for the world, the values of poetry must be accepted. Although less materialistic than the eighteenth century, his own time seemed prosaic. It felt little need for intellectual and spiritual knowledge.[1]

The poem "Youth and Manhood" combines this feeling of the world's indifference with the poet's sense of being aloof from material struggles. But he suspects that his youth may be the reason for his inhabiting a freer, loftier region; the men who plod and think routinely may simply have lost faith with youth. The toil that "indurates the hand" also hardens the heart until it can have no part in "the ideal land." Arrogantly the young poet asks for early achievement and early death: "Give me to chant one pure and deathless lay,/And let me die." When he asked himself why he did not write more poetry, he again emphasized this general indifference: "the world, in its worldliness, does not miss/What the poet sings." Since the writer in objectifying his thought, or dream, has cast it away from him, silence may be preferable to song (*Poems*, 24-26, 45).

Allied with this uncertainty about poetry was a feeling that "Too broad a daylight wraps us all," that richness and mystery were lost when too much was explained. Perhaps uncertain of his own beliefs, he was nonetheless convinced that reverie and intuition and introspection lost much when forced into the semireality of words. Few men, in fact, understood or valued meditation. He resented the fact that the world would in such cases "dub thee idler, smiling sneeringly," although they were occupied only with a "busy vacancy"; he desired occasionally, with a friend, to build "A wall of quiet thought, and gentle books/ Betwixt us and the hard and bitter world." Yet this retirement was not in itself sufficient, for he also believed that a private art intended for the few was an imperfect and largely useless art.[2]

II *Early Criticism*

When he began publishing critical prose essays in *Russell's,* Timrod was still aware of these conflicts. Hayne suggests that his first work, "The Character and Scope of the Sonnet," was written primarily to defend the form and also Wordsworth "against the assaults of a large body of depreciators." The essay begins uncompromisingly. There is, first, an aristocratic disdain of popular taste. The sonnet "has never been a popular form of verse"; it is never likely to be. But the popularity and the comprehension of a poet's work rarely begin with the multitude. A few cultivated persons understand and explain his work; gradually, after these explanations seep downward, his verses may become popular.

Timrod makes no attempt to reconcile this doctrine with his belief that the poet must speak what men dimly feel but can not say for themselves. Robert Burns is the single exception to this rule, and most people prefer a song of Moore's to the finest sonnet.

Timrod also slashes at Samuel Rogers for saying that he would never allow himself to be tied down to fourteen lines, but it was excellent for Wordsworth as "its strict limits prevented him from lapsing into that diffuseness to which he was prone." The sonnet, like the Spenserian stanza, was the invention of a poet "of happy taste; and this little harp of fourteen strings, after having been swept with great effect by the hands of a few masters, has been accepted and approved as one of the legitimate instruments of poetry."

The sonnet has been called artificial. Timrod cheerfully admits this, but he claims that

> It *is* artificial, but only as all forms of verse are artificial. There are persons who imagine poetry to be the result of a sort of mystical inspiration, scarcely to be subjected to the bounds of space and time. Others regarding it as the outgushing of a present emotion, cannot conceive how the poet, carried on by the "divine afflatus," should always contrive to rein in his Pegasus at a certain goal. All this is simply ridiculous. If the poet have his hour of inspiration (though we are so sick of the cant of which this word has been the fruitful source, that we dislike to use it) it is not during the act of composition. A distinction must be made between the moment when the great thought first breaks upon the mind,
>
> > ————— "leaving in the brain
> > A rocking and a ringing,"
>
> and the hour of patient and elaborate execution. It is in the conception only that the poet is the *vates*. In the labor of putting that conception into words, he is simply the artist. A great poet has defined poetry to be "emotion recollected in tranquillity." No man with grief in his heart, could sit straightway down to strain that grief through iambics. No man, exulting in a delirium of joy, ever bubbles in anapaests. Were this so, the poet would be the most wonderful of improvisators; and, perhaps, poetry would be no better than what improvisations usually are.

That the sonnet is one of the more difficult forms means that it presents a greater challenge to the artist. The enforced condensation requires him to order his thought before he writes: to discard the irrelevant and to concentrate on "one leading idea, around which the others are grouped for purposes of illustration only." Since great poetry had been written in the sonnet form, Timrod, a traditionalist, believed that the form was good: the particular result depended upon the individual poet.[3]

The article on the sonnet may have been provoked only by his reading. It defends the validity of a specific poetic form; except for the significant remarks on art and inspiration, it does not go beyond that. But the second article resulted from violent oral argument in the backroom of John Russell's bookshop, and was a direct rebuttal to the article his adversary had prepared. The first, a defense of neoclassicism, was written by William J. Grayson; the second, by Timrod. Both essays are entitled "What is Poetry?" This has led at least two unwary biographers to quote from Grayson and to attribute the remarks to Timrod, thus making Timrod apparently say exactly the opposite of what he believed.

Grayson's phrasing is salty and diverting. He was defending Dryden and Pope, but he was better on the offense. He particularly disliked Wordsworth and Coleridge, feeling that they beclouded every issue that they touched. Grayson thought of himself as an advocate of common sense—as a follower in criticism of Samuel Johnson and of the Scottish philosophers, especially of Hugh Blair. To Grayson, Wordsworth was

> a sort of verse making machine all his life. He lived to manufacture verses. His morning and evening walks were taken to levy poetical black mail from every stock and stone, every shrub and flower, every bird and butterfly.—The daisy that to Peter Bell was a daisy and nothing more, was to Wordsworth a very different and much more important object—it was a peg to hang verses upon. He turned over every pebble in his path to see if there might not be a stanza lurking beneath it. If he sat down on an occasional bench it produced a poem. If he visited a river it was made to rhyme. If he returned to its banks it was forced to do double duty. . . . He looked on nature as a kind of poetical milch cow, which he was never tired of milking.

Grayson also thought that a reader would more readily believe Coleridge's poem if the ancient mariner had seized upon the unfortunate listener "not before, but after the festival, when being filled with wine and wassail, the maudlin carouser would have been a fit, and perhaps a willing auditor, to the lunatic old Salt." [4] These remarks may not be fair, but they have their amusing points.

Timrod disagreed also with Grayson's concept of poetry. The disagreement, at least superficially, was one of definition. Grayson was a neoclassicist; Timrod, a romantic. Grayson was inclined to answer his question by considering the form; Timrod, by considering the essence or principle of poetry. The argument is in no sense a new one. Aristotle attempted to differentiate between essence and form at a time when the word "poetry" included practically all imaginative writing; with the delimitation of the word in English usage, and with no accepted word to signify the older, larger concept, confusion still results. When the scientist Joseph Le Conte discussed the nature of poetry, he began by carefully considering the dual nature of the term. The form is verse. In essence, prose addresses only the emotions and the understanding; poetry addresses also the imagination and the aesthetic sense. There can be no clear line of demarcation: although lacking the form, much prose is in essence poetry; and much verse, despite its formal quality, is not poetry.

Grayson allowed only the single meaning. Paraphrasing Dr. Johnson, he declared poetry to be "rythmical composition and a poet, one who composes in measure." The peculiar quality of poetry is in the form of arranging words, without regard to the ideas expressed. All other definitions lead to confusion. To him the terms "prose poems" and "poetic prose" seemed "as incongruous as the phrases, round square and oblong circle." Such phrases were simply a "mystical jargon of rapturous superlatives" freely used by the "transcendental oracular school" of Coleridge and his followers. They sought to give to poetry qualities that poetry did not have. An example of this was in Coleridge's defining poetry "as the proper antithesis not of prose but of science. What more is this than to insist on using words contrary to their common acceptation? According to general usage, is not art the proper antithesis of science?" Also, is it not enough to be a good poet, when poetry itself "is the noblest, most refined, pointed and energetic of the two modes by which among all people, thought and emotion are expressed by language?"

By Grayson's standards, all verse is poetry. A casual bit of doggerel belongs to the genre as surely as the finest work of Milton or Shakespeare. Once this is allowed, the province of inquiry changes: from asking what it is, one must turn to an examination of the quality of a poem. Here, figurative language may be used effectively, but the labelling of a poem as "prosy" does not mean that the work is prose; it means simply that the writer was a clumsy poet. The intrinsic merit can be judged, but the simple and clear distinction between poetry and prose must remain steadfast.

Grayson's essay infuriated Timrod. He objected particularly

to the "illogical confusion of the ideas conveyed by the terms *poem,* and *poetry*," which Grayson had used as identical in reference. A poem is objective, tangible, a thing complete within itself; poetry is subjective, an essence of feeling rather than a definable reality. Then the antithesis to prose becomes, properly, metre; if this is recognized, the question ceases to be how to distinguish poetry from prose, and becomes an inquiry into "those operations of the human faculties, which, when *incarnated* in language, are generally recognized as poetry."

A part of the definition, therefore, turns on the character of the poet. He must have "a more than ordinary sensibility," and out of this characteristic must come a "medium of strong emotion" which can fuse and transform the objects and thoughts which are the material of poetry. From this powerfully emotional imagination there comes naturally a language which differs from the language of prose. The poet's words are sensuous, picturesque, and impassioned; they are short and concrete. Although the thought may be abstract, the poetic expression of that thought must have life, form, and color. Abstract words make the verse prosaic, until the work "no longer calls up the image which it expresses; it merely suggests the thought which it stands for." The poet is not content with words that convey the meaning; he seeks also the most beautiful, in sound and in association, so that his words will "challenge a slight attention to themselves."

The form is important, but it is not all-inclusive. Timrod is willing to admit that "there may be such a thing as a prose-poem." Yet he admits it reluctantly. Concentrated, heightened thought and emotion find their natural and proper expression in verse. In a long poem, certain parts will inevitably be merely skillful verse, but the artistry of the writer must so fuse these passages with the impassioned poetry that the entire work will be an organic whole.

As criticism, Timrod's essay suffers from being a rebuttal as well as an affirmation. The lines of the argument had been drawn in unshaded black and white by another man; they outraged Timrod's sense of the philosophical and the mystical, which he felt to be at the heart of poetry; but the narrow matter-of-factness of the preceding argument made a reasoned answer difficult. He was forced to deny rather than to disprove. The most valuable part of his reply is in the place that he could most tangibly take hold of his adversary's dicta: in the matter of poetic language. Significantly, in these statements Timrod is on the side of Dante, and not of Wordsworth. He declares that words in themselves have beauty and euphony and concreteness; in this, he answers Grayson convincingly.[5]

Timrod also disagreed flatly with Grayson's judgment of individual poets. Grayson's idea of common sense in poetry seemed "to be conceived very much in the spirit of Charles Lamb's literal Scotchman." Certainly there were few points of resemblance between Coleridge's "philosophical notion of common sense" and Grayson's quibbling and niggling definition.

The attack on Coleridge Timrod could take calmly; that on Wordsworth was another matter: "Of the caricature of Wordsworth it is difficult to speak without indignation." Timrod's rejoinder is not exactly calm. He denied indignantly that Wordsworth had a mechanical view of nature, or that he used it for ulterior purposes; on the contrary, "Perhaps no poet ever felt so deeply, certainly none has ever described so admirably, that complete abandonment of the soul to the influence of Nature, in which 'Thought is not; in enjoyment it expires.'" He quoted from "Tintern Abbey" to prove that Wordsworth was not "a coxcomb, who traded with Nature for his poetry," but a man who in fitting language "depicts those moods of ecstatic contemplation, in which the soul, through a faculty not dependent upon the senses, feels the presence of that mysterious and universal, of which the world is a manifestation." Wordsworth had occasionally been guilty, as Coleridge conceded, of matter-of-factness. This consisted in "an occasional, and somewhat superfluous, minuteness of detail," but this occasional (not general) blemish arose from the poet's intense desire to "bring the groupings and situations of his few characters distinctly before the mind of the reader." To offset this, Timrod lists over a dozen poems that reveal Wordsworth's "powers of imaginative description" (*Essays*, 78-80).

Timrod's third and last article in *Russell's* was apparently first delivered as a lecture. The printed version is entitled "Literature in the South." It is only one of many similar articles, but with accuracy Jay B. Hubbell calls it the "most penetrating analysis of the difficulties of the Southern author."[6] Certainly a vast amount of Southern intellectual energy was expended, in the years 1830-60, in presenting arguments and pleas for a regional intellectual independence. These partisan efforts to create a literary nationalism brought little in the way of tangible results. If the discussion was unprofitable, the problem itself was painful, engrossing, and apparently inescapable.

To this forensic arena of bitterness and vexation, Timrod came late. By 1859 the South was almost unified in its opposition to the North. The easy, popular thing to do was to throw hard verbal bricks at Boston and New York. Timrod does his share of throwing, but he does not absolve his own region of blame or responsibility. The Southern author is "the Pariah of modern literature" because he is caught between hostility and contempt abroad and scornful indifference at home: "It is the settled conviction of the North that genius is indigenous there, and flourishes only in a Northern atmosphere. It is the equally firm conviction of the South that genius—literary genius, at least—is an exotic that will not flower on a Southern soil."

Timrod reserves his sharpest thrusts for Southerners. Native writers are neglected because literature is considered an epicurean amusement, and because readers prefer classical and neoclassical to the modern, romantic authors. The writer himself is not esteemed in a land where taste is archaic and judgment is uninformed. Timrod never doubted the superiority of nineteenth-century writing; he was troubled only that readers and teachers seemed frequently to prefer Pope to Wordsworth and remained oblivious to "that most important revolution in imaginative literature . . . which took place a little more than half a century ago." The men who brought about that revolution had introduced a mystical element into verse, which distinguished it from earlier kinds; and into criticism they brought an analysis which deduced its laws from nature and truth rather than from the authority of particular writers.

Equally provincial and almost equally harmful was the current demand from another group for a superficial "Southernism in literature." It closely resembled the earlier demand for "Americanism in literature," and each meant only that "an author should confine himself in the choice of his subjects to the scenery, the history, and the traditions" of his own section or country. Without any qualification, Timrod labeled this a false, narrow criterion by which to judge of true nationality. It is in the han-

dling of a subject, and not in the subject itself, that the characteristics of a writer are revealed; and "he alone, who, in a style
evolved from his own individual genius, speaks the thoughts and
feelings of his own deep heart, can be a truly national genius."
To such a writer, the circumscription of subjects was foolish and
unfortunate. The author must have the right to choose according
to his own needs and taste; that he would not thereby lose his
nationality was easily proved by the Roman plays of Shakespeare and the French novels of Scott.

The remedy must come through a change in education and
in criticism. Too many schools and colleges still considered the
works of Hugh Blair and Lord Kames as possessing "unquestion-
able authority." Literary criticism was even more backward:
"Here no one is surprised when some fossil theory of criticism,
long buried under the ruins of an exploded school, is dug up,
and discussed with infinite gravity by gentlemen who know
Pope and Horace by heart, but who have never read a word of
Wordsworth or Tennyson, or who have read them with suspicion,
and rejected them with superciliousness." These men are bigots.
Equally bad are those who are slaves to English or Northern
critical authority, and those who consider validity in literature
as "a mere matter of taste." It is good, Timrod admits, to be
independent. Yet "some respect is certainly due to the authority
of those who, by a careful and loving study of literature, have
won the right to speak *ex cathedra.* Nor is that independence,
but license, which is not founded upon a wide and deep knowledge of critical science, and upon a careful and respectful col-
lation of our own conclusions, with the impartial philosophical
conclusions of others" (*Essays,* 85-87).

The greatest difficulty of all is the general attitude toward
creative writers and writing, by which the "novel and the poem
are almost universally characterized as light reading, and we
may say are almost universally estimated as a very light and
superficial sort of writing" (91). Before the South could have a
great literature, the intellectual climate had to be changed and
vivified. Good work had to be ungrudgingly recognized, as it
had not been in the past:

> Of all our Southern writers, not one but Poe has received his
> due measure of fame. The immense resources and versatile
> powers of Simms are to this day grudgingly acknowledged, or

contemptuously denied. There have been writers among us who, in another country, would have been complimented with repeated editions, whose names are now almost forgotten, and whose works it is now utterly impossible to obtain. While our centre-tables are littered with the feeble moralizings of Tupper, done up in very bright morocco; and while the corners of our newspapers are graced with the glibly versified common-places of Mackey, and of writers even more worthless than Mackey, there is, perhaps, scarcely a single bookseller in the United States, on whose face we should not encounter the grin of ignorance, if we chanced to inquire for the Froissart ballads of Philip Pendleton Cooke (96-97).

The South had to be jarred out of its self-complacency with rude truths and even with satire directed against slavish or antiquated critics and against an outmoded system of education. Then, and only then, "we may look for a literature of which we shall all wear the honors" (102).

There is a small amount of good if incidental criticism in Timrod's letters. In response to his sister's query, he pronounced *Villette* inferior to *Jane Eyre* and *Shirley,* but in all three he greatly admired Charlotte Brontë's "skill in sky and weather-painting." [7] In a letter to Rachel Lyons, and probably because of her recommendation, he noted that he had read with great pleasure *Beulah,* by "your friend Miss Evans." It was a "very clever work," but without any special excellence or "any marked originality in the style and characters of the story." Augusta Jane Evans had been praised for her philosophical speculations, but the book only revealed that she had read a great deal of philosophy and had been puzzled and bewildered by it. This resulted in the greatest defect in the novel: "Beulah's transition from scepticism to Faith is left almost wholly unaccounted for." For Miss Evans' "theory of poetical genius" imbedded in the novel, Timrod had only contempt: "I think it would not be difficult to show that Poetry is *not* merely a noble *insanity;* and that the errors and eccentricities of poets have not been *in consequence* of, but *in spite* of the influence of the poetical temperament. In fact, the poet, in his completest development, involves the metaphysician, and is a more sound, wholesome, and perfect human being, than the gravest of those utterers of half-truths who set up as philosophers." [8]

Even brotherly affection could not bring him to pardon bad

poetry: "Sissie [Edyth] has been sending me several sheets of her nonsense. Poor girl! She has very little to amuse her, and I found it hard to tell her the truth about them. But of all things in the world, I think a poetaster the most contemptible; and to save myself the discredit of having one for a sister, I have written to her, treating her versicles without mercy." This brutal letter has not survived, nor is there any known copy of his sister's verses.[9]

In his longest and best essay, "A Theory of Poetry," [10] Timrod develops and completes his earlier attempts at definition. After dismissing briefly Grayson's essay, he considers Poe's dogmatic statements that a long poem is a contradiction in terms and that the poetical sentiment is derived only from the sense of the beautiful.

In response to the first dictum, Timrod presents two answers. One has to do with the reading of poetry. Although a psychic excitement is necessarily transient, it does not follow that poetry must be read in that mood. In fact, the reading of the greatest poetry "is characterized . . . by a thoughtful sublimity and the matured and almost inexhaustible strength of a healthy intellect." Granted this quality of mind, the reader need not complete a poem at one sitting to preserve its unity of effect. If he reads the first book of *Paradise Lost,* he will bring to the second and third books all the impressions of his former reading; he will feel a deeper richness as he continues. The mind will be conscious of the vast unity of the poem, so that "its grand purport and harmonious proportions become more and more clearly apparent."

The length of a poem has nothing to do with its excellence. Only the author can know how long a poem should be; and only through "the ordeal of criticism" can the author's success or failure be determined. Timrod admits that he is inclined to consider Dante's *Divine Comedy* as three distinct poems and Spenser's *Faerie Queene* as a succession of poems. The character of the poem and the intention of the poet may be responsible for a lack of unity. But the poet, if he has artistry enough, can impose order and secure unity. Not all of his poem will in the subjective sense be genuine poetry; parts of it will inevitably be verse, but "these parts may be raised so far above the ordinary level of prose by skillful verse as to preserve the general harmony of the poem and materially to insure its unity as a work of art" (*Essays,* 112-13).

From Poe's theory that poetry was limited in subject to "the sense of the beautiful," Timrod dissented vigorously. He was willing to grant the validity of this kind of poetry, and even to admit that Poe had "fixed with some definiteness one phase of its merely subjective manifestation. It is, indeed, to the inspiration which lies in the ethereal, the remote and the unknown, that the world owes some of its sweetest poems; and the poetry of words has never so strange a fascination as when it seems to suggest more than it utters." But to admit the validity of the kind was not to accept this kind as the only, or even the highest, poetry. Literature is not independent of life or of truth. The creation of beauty is a sufficient aim for a writer; it is not the highest or noblest aim.

Essentially, Timrod was an ethical critic. He did not propose to limit the scope of poetry, but he was convinced that the greatest verse must have an ethical content. Poe had attempted to reduce the many and varied sources of poetry to a single element: beauty. There are other, equally valid sources: particularly, power and truth. A poem need not be philosophical, but it can embody philosophy; every poet has the right "to make his art the vehicle of great moral and philosophical lessons" (*Essays*, 117-18).

Milton had successfully embodied in a poem Truth, Power, and Beauty. Poe failed to recognize this coalition because he ignored his own distinction between poetry and a poem, between the spirit and its body. Timrod added: "I hold that the confusion of these terms, of the subjective essence with the objective form, is the source of most of the errors and contradictions of opinion prevalent upon this subject." The essence need not be expressed through words; it could take form as music, painting, or any other art. The poem was different. Through words the author must give objective form to the subjective essence: "I look upon every poem as strictly a work of art, and on the Poet, in the act of putting poetry into verse, simply as an artist" (*Essays*, 119). He lifted a passage on inspiration from his article on the sonnet, revised and expanded it somewhat, but only in order to state more forcibly his conviction that good poems are never improvisations.

Timrod had no wish to denigrate earlier poetry; in fact, he was pleading for a wider, more all-embracing theory that would include all forms of poetry. Yet he was also convinced that Wordsworth had introduced something new and valuable: "These were, first, that the material and stimulants of poetry might be found in some of the commonest things about us, and second that behind the sights, sounds and hues of external Nature, there is 'something more than meets the senses, something undefined and unutterable which must be felt and perceived by the soul' in its moments of rapt contemplation. It is this latter feeling that constitutes the originality of Wordsworth." It is not to be found, asserted Timrod, in Shakespeare and his contemporaries, or in Milton, Dryden, Pope, Thomson, or Cowper; it appeared "for the first time in literature, in the lines of Wordsworth written near Tintern Abbey. Since then it has been caught up and shadowed forth in every shape by every poet from Byron to the present English Laureate [Tennyson]." Wordsworth was the best of modern poets (*Essays*, 124-27).

His closest rival was Tennyson. In some respects his vision was broader than Wordsworth's. Tennyson could see the truth of Poe's contention that in a certain poem the poet "may aim at beauty alone," but he could also see the truth of Wordsworth's contention that the high office of a poet made it necessary for him to combine within himself "thinker, seer, teacher, and bard" (*Essays*, 129). For Tennyson, beauty alone was not always enough: "not the less does he recognize the right of the poet to make his art the vehicle of great moral and philosophical lessons, not less does he recognize his right to grapple with the darkest problems of man's destiny, to discuss the fears and perplexities of the spirit, and the faith which triumphs over them, and even to drop now and then, a silken line into the dim sea of metaphysics" (*Essays*, 130).

Timrod has words of high praise for Mathew Arnold, but he thinks his poetic theory wrongfully narrow. Equally crippling would be one that might be drawn from the work of the Brownings, admirable as he considered their poetry to be. Byron and Moore were not enough, especially in the love poems in which "a woman is in the same breath addressed as an angel, and wooed as the frailest of sinners." A creed that justified only one type of poetry was not inclusive enough, for such creeds have generally "grown out of the idiosyncrasies of the poets themselves, and so necessarily seldom attain a greater breadth than suffices to shelter the theorist and the models from which he has drawn his arguments and his inspirations. . . . That certainly can be no true poetical creed which leads directly to the neglect of those masterpieces which though wrought hundreds or thousands of years ago, still preserve the freshness of their perennial youth." It is necessary to recognize that there are many valid ways of writing because "there are no stereotyped forms of poetry" (*Essays*, 128-31).

III *As Editor*

After Timrod became an editor of the Columbia *Daily South Carolinian* in January, 1864, it was part of his task to prepare a couple of editorials or "dwarf essays" for each issue. Many of them seem to have been casually done, but quite a few are thoughtful. An early one was addressed "To Our Poetical Contributors." This was a public performance; also, it may be, Timrod had mellowed somewhat in his opinion of mere versifiers. Whatever the reason, he begins mildly. But the concluding sentences are, under their politeness, as uncompromising as words can well be:

> We have a heart to sympathise with all lovers of poetry, not excepting those who are incompetent to appreciate it critically, and who, in consequence, sometimes, mistake its weeds for its flowers. The instinct which leads all men to delight in the musical expression of sentiment is a divine one, and we may not despise it even where its action happens to be vitiated by defects of judgment and taste. Such, indeed, is our reverence for that instinct, that we are inclined to accord some respect even to the writer of bad verse. Indifferent rhyme may occasionally be the offspring of genuine feeling, for poetry is an art in which no one can excel without genius and cultivation. Where, then, the offender has the excuse of natural emotion, we think he ought to be treated with great gentleness. Yet, at the same time, we would advise all in whom the *aura divina* is wanting, to suppress their productions, however unaffected may have been the impulse which led to these compositions. There is no necessity of giving to the public verses, the only merit of which is in the source from which they spring. With regard to the poetical criminal whose inspiration is vanity alone, we have no mercy for him whatever. There ought to be a pillory for the punishment of every evil-doer of this stamp.

We may as well state at the outset, that the standard upon which we have fixed, and by which we shall measure all poetical contributions to our columns, is high, and that to that standard we shall adhere, without reference to any other considerations than those of merit or demerit. While there are in the English language so many exquisite poems not very well known, we shall prefer to give selections from these, or even from authors who, however familiar, can never lose their perennial freshness, than to afflict our critical readers with such effusions as, in the corner of some newspapers, appear under the head of original verse. [11]

One who reads today the poetry that Timrod included in his columns may feel that he frequently relaxed his standards. But he was publishing, or quite often reprinting, the work of people whom he knew personally. In addition to his own and some of his father's work, Timrod used many poems by his friends: Hayne, Simms, Bruns, and Requier; several by two men—Harry Lyndon Flash and James Ryder Randall—whom he had met in his days as war correspondent; a poem by Thomas Bailey Aldrich and part of one by Whittier; and quotations from many English poets. He felt himself unduly handicapped: he could not pay for original contributions, and he did not himself receive the papers that came to the office. Even his opportunity to clip and reprint was limited.[12]

In January, 1864, Timrod began to write a series of editorials that continue and in part repeat his essay "Literature in the South." He did not believe that "the nationality of the South" dated from the commencement of the Civil War. It had been slowly developing over a long period; through

the effect of time, distance, diversity of soil and climate, opposition of interests and antagonistic traits, habits, sentiments, opinions and institutions, the Yankee and the Southerner became ultimately as far removed, in every particular, from each other, as the Englishman is from the Frenchman.

It is in these facts that the future philosophic historian will seek the true causes of secession. Abolition and the tariff were little more than the occasions of that movement.[13]

Along with its many evils, the war had brought about one improvement: the blockade had cut off the supply of English and Northern books, and thus had forced Southerners to read native works. In turn, Southern authors, awake "to the fact that they have at last an audience," had been writing vigorously and with enough ability to indicate "that a new era of intellectual energy is dawning upon us." These books and the best of the literary magazine and papers show "the national mind struggling to find fit and original expression." If there is much imitation and many indifferent books, there is also evidence that Southern literature is beginning to "trust to its native strength alone." [14]

Although he favored an independence of foreign models and asked for a literature that would reflect and reveal the Southern mind, Timrod did not want a local-color literature. He rephrases his earlier concept: "There is but one way to be a truly national writer, and that is by being a truly original writer . . . the man of original genius draws his matter from the depth of his own being; and the national character, in which, as a unit of the nation, he shares, finds its utterance through him." [15]

Timrod also considered the parallel demand for a national song. Most songs of this kind he thought worthless from a literary point of view. "The Star-Spangled Banner" and "Rule Britannia" gained popularity through their effective refrains, and not through any merit as poetry; with the exception of "Maryland, My Maryland," no Southern song attained even that type of popularity. Since people do not·choose their songs on the basis of poetic merit, the poets were not to blame. Timrod lists four things as necessary to the success of a national song: "Its verse must run glibly on the tongue; it must contain somewhere, either in a stanza or in a refrain, a sentiment, tersely and musically expressed, which appeals to some favorite pride, prejudice, or passion of the people; it must be married to an effective, but not complicated air, and it must be aided by such a collocation of accidents as may not be computed." The poet even of genius cannot control all of these elements; the Confederacy possessed no writers equal to the task of expressing "the whole great soul of a nation within the compass of a few simple and melodious verses." But the task was worth attempting, and he hoped that writers would, in the effort, "find inspiration enough to draw forth the utmost capacity of their genius." [16]

He was not optimistic. The turbulence and excitement of war might be excellent as a period of germination but not as one of growth. Yet the intense emotion which prevents a poet from writing well at the time may give strength and character to his thought. After a period of meditation, which could come only with the return of peace, Southern writers might be able to write great poems.[17]

Many nonliterary editorials quote from or allude to Timrod's favorite poets. In an untitled editorial he contrasts English materialism with the ethereal enchantment of Spenser, and English narrowness of policy with Shakespeare's universal sympathies.[18] He levied tribute frequently also on Wordsworth and on Robert Burns. Only a few editorials deal directly with the war. The best is "The Grandeur of the Struggle." It was easy, he noted, to be too conscious of human meanness, selfishness, cowardice, and crime, and to overlook or forget the valor, self-sacrifice, patience, determination, and patriotism that were "around us." [19] Perhaps the most moving is his account of the plight of South Carolinian refugees, especially those from the southeastern seaboard whose entire region had been conquered. Timrod had taught at Bluffton and at Hardeeville, and he writes with warm compassion of people that he had known well.[20]

Hayne reprinted three editorials from texts supplied by Mrs. Timrod; he notes that they appeared in the *South Carolinian*, but gives no dates. The first is a romantic tribute to the Confederate raider "Alabama," recently sunk in the English Channel after circumnavigating the globe and after having destroyed many Northern ships. The second, "Spring's Lessons," was written after Appomattox. It is good that spring is not subject to radical rule, for she would be outlawed "by Thaddeus Stevens and his crew. For Spring is a true reconstructionist," bringing beauty and calm and hope to a devastated region. In the third, Timrod fancies that he can find in the sound of each month's name the characteristics of that particular month. It merits Hayne's epithet of "poetic prose," but little more.[21]

These represent Timrod at his editorial best. A few are impressive; most of them suffer, as he felt that his poetry suffered, from the lack of tranquillity. Also, the work was somewhat mixed, if not downright chaotic, as he described it to Hayne: "I have not written a line of verse for a twelve-month. All the poetry in my Nature has been fagged out of me I fear. I work very hard—besides writing the leaders of the paper I often descend into the local column, as you must have noticed by such articles as *Literary Pranks, Arsenal Hill,* and the *Troubles of a Midsummer Night.* My object is to show that a poet can drudge as well [as] a duller man, and therefore I don't complain." It was one thing to drudge uncomplainingly, and presumably Timrod was equal to that task; it was quite another, under the circumstances, to write with strength and intelligence. Even dwarf essays require a sustained thought that Timrod often seemed unable to give to them.[22]

The most interesting of his postwar criticism he put into letters to Hayne. The two shared a vigorous dislike of the South Carolina poet and critic James Wood Davidson. When Davidson asserted dogmatically that *my* and *thy* should never be used before vowels, but always *mine* and *thine,* Timrod cited three instances when Tennyson used the shorter pronouns, and added: "Even this fool's favorite Poe has 'My Mother, *my own* Mother who died early.' The truth is, of course, that this rule is not, like similar rules in Greek and French, imperative in English. The poet has the privilege of using either form as his ear dictates. Mr. Davidson has no ear, and therefore he cannot understand that if I had crunched together so many *ns* as I would have done if I had written 'in thine unmingled scorn,' so far from consulting the laws of euphony, I should have been guilty of a cacophony. But you know these things as well as I."[23]

The best is also his last-known bit of written criticism. When he received Hayne's prize poem, Timrod assessed it in mild yet exact terms: "I received your prize poem this morning—thank you for sending it. It is a very noble production indeed—quite worthy of the crown—but may I be so frank as to tell you that its excellence seems to me rather rhetorical than poetical. This fault, however, belongs to all prize poems—to mine, I think, in a far greater degree than your own. The poet cannot draw his purest and subtlest strains except from his own unremunerated heart."[24]

CHAPTER 4

Poet of Love and War

I *Lukewarm Secessionist*

TIMROD'S ONETIME TEACHER, W. J. Rivers, wrote after the poet's death: "The terrible realities of our late eventful history, roused him as nothing else could have roused him; and in the excitement of his soul he strung his lyre to more exalted themes and poured forth in quick succession many spirited odes, which give him rank among the foremost lyric poets of America." This statement is mainly true. Timrod is remembered today almost entirely for his war poems, and the progress of the war can be spiritually though not literally traced through his poetry. But Timrod soon hated war in general, and the Civil War in particular.

At the beginning, he was only a lukewarm secessionist. After the war, when he appealed for help to Richard Henry Stoddard, he made it clear that he did not want "to appear before you in a false position. I must premise, therefore, that in the late civil conflict I was a Secessionist in opinion, though the state of my health precluded my bearing arms." Yet there is justification for Hayne's bitter rejoinder to an apparently sarcastic letter from Rossiter Johnson. Hayne states flatly that "Timrod opposed secession. . . . The inference that a man who defends his Country, with pen or sword—against invasion—altho he may have opposed the measures of his People, which led to such invasion—, occupies practically the same position as a man who advocated the war-breeding Policy—, is really so eccentric an idea as to defy all logic and reason. . . . You knew perfectly well when you penned your letter, if you did not know before, that Timrod disapproved Secession, and fought (logically) against it!" [1]

Timrod's letters bear this out, but his early war poems do not.

The first, "Ethnogenesis" (which Timrod called "a sesquipedalian title" and translated as "Birth of a Nation"; apparently he preferred to call it simply "Ode on the Meeting of the Southern Congress"—its first title), was written during the meeting of the first Confederate Congress in Montgomery, Alabama, during February, 1861. It seems to have been issued originally as a broadside; Thompson records that it "was read in public for the first time at a dinner party of distinguished South Carolinians, who were so delighted with it that they made up a handsome purse of gold and sent it to the author as a substantial evidence of their appreciation."

In his poem, Timrod was confident that a new nation was being, or in fact had been, born. A new flag would soon be unfurled in many distant ports. Nature would bring forth crops of grain, but especially the fields (in Timrod's mild but capitalized conceit) would be covered with the snow of Southern summers. To him, as to many men far better versed in economics, cotton would be the protection and the salvation of the South. The North had turned completely materialistic, in doing so had set up an "evil throne, and warred with God," and had become the implacable foe of the new nation. Northern armies might invade it. If so, the South would meet them with memories of Revolutionary victories, with the aid of a fertile soil, and with unfaltering patriotism. Although Timrod later was to write that slavery and the tariff were only incidental causes of secession, in this poem he pictures the North as having turned religion into fanaticism, with "creeds that dare to preach/What Christ and Paul refrained to preach," and as having used schemes that would cause "the neighboring poor/To starve and shiver."

In this irregular Pindaric ode (as he thought of it) Timrod several times uses effectively the Miltonic simile which he so much admired. At least two he combined with the conceit. If God had decreed that the South "must pass a redder sea/Than that which rang to Miriam's holy glee," then God would surely raise a "Moses with his rod." Perhaps the finest simile concludes the poem, where he compares the beneficent new nation to the Gulf Stream:

> . . . the type
> Whereby we shall be known in every land
> Is that vast gulf which lips our Southern strand,

And through the cold, untempered ocean pours
Its genial streams, that far off Arctic shores
May sometimes catch upon the softened breeze
Strange tropic warmth and hints of summer seas.[2]

Closely allied in subject matter, although somewhat removed in time, is Timrod's second Pindaric ode, "The Cotton Boll." Again, this time fundamentally, Timrod celebrates the agricultural, commercial, and diplomatic power of cotton. True, he begins with its beauty, but that is only an introduction. The poet imagines himself reclining under a pine tree, examining a boll of cotton; he looks upon a glowing landscape, for "Although I gaze upon no waste of snow,/The endless field is white." But the charms of the South are already widely known, especially through the works of William Gilmore Simms; with his pencil he has "touched our very swamps with grace." Where, however, is the poet who shall sing of the power of cotton, which brings happiness and wealth to France and England as well as to the South? It is the source of

That mighty commerce which, confined
To the mean channels of no selfish mart,
Goes out to every shore
Of this broad earth, and throngs the sea with ships
That bear no thunders; hushes hungry lips
In alien lands;
Joins with a delicate web remotest strands;

Cotton will guard the new nation's "hearth-stones as a bulwark"; through its kindly power the "half-dead dream of universal peace" may be revived. In a Miltonic simile he compares his own calm writing with the labors of miners in Cornwall, who work on oblivious of roaring storms overhead. He is in the midst of another and more violent storm, for "the quiet summer air/Stirs with the bruit of battles." Although confident of victory and resigned to God's will, he prays for peace since in war there are violence and bloodshed that "even Victory must regret."

Timrod remained prejudiced. The Northern invaders were Goths. Perhaps fortunately, a good poem can have in it remarkably bad prophecy; in the stirring invocation at the end of the poem, Timrod pictures a fate for New York City that has not quite materialized:

Oh, help us, Lord! to roll the crimson flood
Back on its course, and, while our banners wing
Northward, strike with us! till the Goth shall cling
To his own blasted altar-stones, and crave
Mercy; and we shall grant it, and dictate
The lenient future of his fate
There, where some rotting ships and crumbling quays
Shall one day mark the Port which ruled the Western seas.[3]

At the very time he was writing so confidently, Timrod was
unhappy and depressed; he sent to Rachel Lyon a sonnet "by
way of illustrating the dark moods which have not seldom
visited me during this infernal summer." As he presents it, this
state was not caused by any definite grief or pain: "I know
not why, but all this weary day,/Sad fancies have been flitting
through my brain." He was not happy with his tutorial work;
he wanted to enlist but realized that he had too little physical
strength to make a good soldier; he was uneasily conscious that
over the martial "lyre of Tyrtaeus . . . I have but small command." [4] He was, finally, troubled by uncertainty in love. He
confessed to Emily that he no longer loved Sophie Sosnowski,
but he was fascinated by Katie Goodwin, whom he had once
regarded as the equivalent of a cousin, and increasingly by the
beautiful, witty, and keen-minded Jewish girl, Rachel Lyons.

II *Love Poems*

For Katie he wrote in December of 1861 a long poem in
rhymed couplets that has since become the most popular of his
love poems. Apparently it was unpremeditated. He wrote to
Rachel that the "Goddess knocked at the door of my study last
Saturday night and handed me a poem entitled 'Katie'!" But he
cautioned Rachel not to take the sentiments expressed too
literally, since "Katie and I are by no means on the lover-like
terms implied in my verse. . . . If you ask me why then should
I address her in so passionate a style, I can only answer that
(metrically) I am always in love for the time with the woman
who forms the subject of my song. It is a species of hallucina-
tion for which I shall not here attempt to account." [5]
In the poem, after paying tribute to Katie's "foreign grace"—
English charm and air—Timrod imagines meeting her on the

street of Bury St. Edmunds, birthplace of Katie and the shrine of the king and martyr. In fancy he strolls with her through English lanes, admiring the countryside, listening to the sound of the birds, and remembering the history of the town and of the ancient ruined abbey. Together they go to the younger church, already old before the Pilgrims sailed for America. In that church Katie had learned the creed, and possibly something more: the ability to flirt. So he imagines that it is he, not Katie, who is the foreigner, until the South Carolina landscape looks English, and in his native Broad River he seems to hear the Larke. From England then "We'll cleave the sea with wings of steam," until soon, beneath the groves of palm, kind friends would greet the "Southron and his English bride." [6]

It is not a cousinly poem. Yet he objected with some justice when Rachel Lyons called the poem Byronic and specifically compared a couplet from "Katie" with one from "Parasina":

The *thoughts* have no resemblance whatever. Byron in Parasina is simply speaking of the peculiar effects of twilight on wave and leaf; while the "greener hues" and "deeper blues" of "Katie" derive their greater intensity from the imaginative eye of love. I only make use of the same words as Byron, on the principle that two painters make use of the same colours; but my tree is not Byron's tree, nor is my sky the sky which looks down upon Hugo and Parasina. Besides the couplet in my poem is made the text of a train of sentiment which is much more *Wordsworthian* than Byronic in its character; and the *tones* of the two paragraphs in which the several couplets occur are as much opposed to each other as the climate of England is to the climate of Italy. [7]

Possibly to propitiate her because she seemed inclined to "hand me over to Katie," Timrod soon wrote a poem to and for Rachel. It is a richer and better poem; in fact, it is the best of his love poems. Rachel is infinitely more complex than Katie. Sometimes her brows wear "a too imperial air"; she disguises mysterious, eastern thoughts in her dark eyes. Timrod deftly works in a series of biblical allusions to explain and illustrate her racial inheritance. When she plays the piano, he hears the sea avenging "Israel's wrong,/And on the wind floats Miriam's song." Successively she suggests to him—by one or another attribute or mien—royal Esther, or Ruth talking to Naomi or lying at the feet of Boaz. He reverses the final image for his conclusion: soon he will be stretched at her feet. The conclusion is merely gallant, but the lyrical portrait of a complex woman makes "La Belle Juive" otherwise a satisfying poem.

About this time Timrod wrote in Rachel's diary some lines that she was free to show "to whom you please, but unless I should choose to print them, I do not wish anybody to possess them but yourself. As yet, I think them only the germ of a good poem." These are probably "Lines to R. L.," which Hayne included in the section "Additional Poems" in the new revised edition. If so, Timrod was wise not to publish them. The opening sentence is a flagrant imitation of Tennyson: "That which we are and shall be is made up/Of what we have been." The heart, like the earth, has its strata, and contains "Its past within its present." Rachel is not excluded: if the poet could understand her smile, know her griefs, and read her eyes, he would know her true story better than if he had her journal in his hand.[8]

Rachel was friendly but not encouraging. Timrod turned back to Katie. By April of 1862 they were engaged, and Timrod wrote a somewhat uninspired poem, "An Exotic," again emphasizing her English qualities. She was at one moment Tudor Elizabeth and at the next a frank, loving girl, whose low reply caused him to walk "from the porch with the tread of a king,/And she was a queen again!"[9]

III *War Poems*

In the winter of 1862 Timrod was spurred to write at least two war poems by the threatened spring invasion of the South and especially of South Carolina. On February 6, he wrote to Rachel Lyons: "I suppose you saw my 'Cry to Arms,' but to make sure I enclose a copy of the poem. I have another and a far better poem behind—addressed to Carolina particularly—which I am meanly keeping back in order to make as good a bargain as I can." Certainly "A Cry to Arms" and "Carolina" have several elements in common. Each is an appeal to men to leave all other tasks to join in the defense of their homeland. The first deals with the entire Confederacy; the second, with the specific state. Each is optimistic of success, provided that

Southern men fight to their utmost. For each poem assumes that Northern armies will be the invaders; they are respectively despots who rove "your fairest lands" and who tread "thy sacred sands"; they are tyrants and they are Huns. Nonetheless, they bid fair to be victorious, if the new nation or the old state dallies complacently.[10]

The themes are similar, but the poetic method and structures are not. "A Cry to Arms" has a conventional eight-line stanza, with alternate rhymes and an alternating four- and three-foot line; even the declaratory "Ho!" in the first and last stanzas does not function by itself, but is made part of a regular foot. Yet Timrod gives this resonant lyric a poetic artistry, even a certain indirection, by the use of conceits. Hayne did not like this poetic device, but he thought the poem contained "one of the few palpable conceits I can recall, which would seem not merely admissable, but charming." I believe now that he referred to the last two stanzas, in which the Lily (the Southern woman) "calmly braves the storm"; why then should the palm-tree (man) have any fear. Some years ago, I thought otherwise.

There are two other conceits in the poem; since they are typical examples of the kind that Timrod used, they may be worth quoting. After calling on men to leave their ordinary tasks, he demands that they "feed your country's sacred dust/ With floods of crimson rain." The other, which may well be the one that the sentimental Hayne had in mind, is by no means intricate:

> Does any falter? let him turn
>   To some brave maiden's eyes,
> And catch the holy fires that burn
>   In those sublunar skies.

"Carolina" has no indirection whatever. The structure is even simpler: three rhyming tetrameter lines, followed by the single-word refrain, "Carolina." It is a battle-cry. The state is in danger. It must be defended. Timrod recalls its colonial and Revolutionary fame; now its sons must unite to repulse a present-day tyrant. The poem became popular immediately, and at least in South Carolina remains so. Roughly ten years later, Hayne remembered that "I read them first, and was thrilled by their power and pathos, upon a stormy March evening in Fort Sumter!

Walking along the battlements, under the red light of a tempestuous sunset, the wind steadily and loudly blowing from off the bar across the tossing and moaning waste of waters, driven inland; with scores of gulls and white sea-birds flying and shrieking round me—those wild voices of Nature mingled strangely with the rhythmic roll and beat of the poet's impassioned music." In 1911 the poem was adopted by the Legislature as the state hymn; after relating this, the mild and scholarly G. A. Wauchope was moved to write: "Emotionally this is the high-water mark of Timrod's poetry. It should never be read except aloud, and it can hardly be sung except standing." [11]

This seems an overstatement. Today readers tend to prefer the poems that record Timrod's disillusionment with war and victory and even with independence. This change is almost directly traceable to Timrod's brief experience in 1862 as a war correspondent and his involvement in the retreat from Shiloh. Perhaps converted by his own words, shortly after writing these two war poems Timrod enlisted. Since Charleston, however, seemed "safe for the present, not indeed in the completeness of its defences, but in the fears of the Yankees," he—as has already been noted earlier—took a three-months leave to act as war correspondent for the Charleston *Mercury*. He had little confidence in his ability to garner news; he went almost entirely, he wrote to Emily, because if he succeeded and made a reputation in that field, he might be able to marry Katie much sooner than he anticipated. He did not succeed. Physically and temperamentally, he was in no way suited to be a war correspondent. He tried hard, but as Rachel Lyons accurately described it, "the work and surroundings were distasteful to him—the hardships, the suffering, the want of congenial associates, all told heavily on his sensitive soul and delicate frame; and yet, there was no complaint, no appeal for sympathy, but a steady adherence to duty." Yet rarely were there any more poems about the glory of feeding the earth with crimson rain. [12]

The hardships had so aggravated his tubercular condition that he returned to Charleston ill. His physician advised him "not to return to camp, but in the absence of any employment, what else can I do?" He did return, but by late October he admitted that he was "totally unfit for camp"; and on December 15, 1862, he was officially discharged from the army. [13]

Even in this trying time, Timrod continued to write some non-war poetry. In November he sent Rachel a letter describing the weariness of having nothing to do in a beleaguered city, but he added that "the muse has not altogether deserted me, as witness the following little serenade which I think you will like, or which you ought to like, at least, for I regard it myself as one of the most perfect small things I have ever done." Timrod's judgment was sound. The two-stanza, sixteen-line "Serenade" is delicate and airy in its evocation of what his sleeping loved one thinks.[14]

It was the beleaguered city, however, that inspired one of his finest and most characteristic poems. Charleston again was threatened with attack from the ocean. The city was calm, the citizens patient and courageous. Charleston had no Gibraltar to guard her, but forts, men, and women waited for the conflict that would inevitably come in the spring. Yet the issue was uncertain. Whether Charleston would remain "fair and free" was a question that could not be answered:

> We know not; in the temple of the Fates
> God has inscribed her doom;
> And, all untroubled in her faith, she waits
> The triumph or the tomb.

Louis Rubin has analyzed this poem, as he himself claims, after the manner of the New Critics. The result is not fully convincing. The poem opens with a simile that Rubin would extend into a metaphor:

> Calm as that second summer which precedes
> The first fall of the snow,
> In the broad sunlight of heroic deeds,
> The City bides the foe.

Rubin would have it that the "city, awaiting attack, stands in the calm light of Indian summer." But the poem has its setting in winter, after the immediate danger of attack was over, not in a mild period in autumn. Until the spring dawns, the city will remain unscathed. The broad sunlight is not physical but figurative: it is the Revolutionary glories of Charleston and of Carolina and of the protecting forts that Timrod is writing of.

The calmness, as Rubin notes, is only on the surface; underneath, there is tension and alertness. The images are grimly warlike, of city and citizens expecting a future attack. They wait, "girt without and garrisoned at home,/Day following patient day"; there are blockade-runners going and coming from Saxon lands along the "tranquil bay." Rubin would extend the metaphor so that it means "far more than a particular Southern city awaiting attack. . . . The pervading tone of regret, of loss, that figures the imagery of 'Charleston' is a commentary on the imminent passing of a civilization." This is true by extension, but it is not implicit in the words or in the imagery. To read "doom" as meaning "destruction," and not in its correct meaning as "fate" (as I feel certain Timrod meant it) is to twist rather than to extend the poem's meaning. "Charleston" is fine enough in its own right that one need not change winter to Indian summer, or tense waiting into a certainty of disaster, to get the full value of the poem.[15]

About the same time Timrod wrote a poem to his friend General Ripley, the "Gay Chieftain" who was mainly responsible for the city's defense. It was uncharacteristic, for it is his only poem to or about an individual soldier. It is not a very good poem, but it may shed some useful light on "Charleston": Timrod sees General Ripley as the leader who shall wield the "weapon of a tyrant's doom." The fate of the enemy is certain; the city will be victorious. The poem is certainly more optimistic than its companion piece, and it is also much shallower; but it indicates that war itself, and not merely defeat, was the destructive force. He made this attitude memorably clear in his next poem, "Christmas."[16]

Both Longfellow and Tennyson admired it. The poem opens with a question, "How grace this hallowed day?" How indeed, in a time of impious war, with crowding memories of friends now dead who were living a year ago; how, when the day should be sacred to "the Prince of Peace"? There was only one fit way: the churches and the people should pray for peace. The poem shifts from questioning and concludes with an invocation to peace, in nature and in life:

> Peace on the whirring marts,
> Peace where the scholar thinks, the hunter roams,
> Peace, God of Peace! peace, peace, in all our homes,
> And peace in all our hearts![17]

Probably at this time, since Timrod was correcting and revising his poems for the anticipated English edition, he also wrote an introductory poem, "Dedication: To K. S. G." As in "Katie," he emphasizes her English traits and calls her "Fair Saxon"; he praises not only England's "undecaying might," but England's insistence on standing always for "truth and right." Here too is one of his finest tributes to the grandeur of English poetry:

> I—who, though born where not a vale
> Hath ever nursed a nightingale,
> Have fed my muse with English song
> Until her feeble wing grew strong—
> Feel, while with all the reverence meet
> I lay this volume at your feet,
> As if through your dear self I pay,
> For many a deep and deathless lay,
> For noble lessons nobly taught,
> For tears, for laughter, and for thought,
> A portion of the mighty debt
> We owe to Shakespeare's England yet! [18]

He also took time out, while winter had brought a partial and temporary cessation to hostilities, to write a prize poem, "Address Delivered at the Opening of the New Theatre at Richmond (1863)." Although he drew heavily and rather effectively on Shakespearean plays for his imagery and made a plea for intellectual and political independence, he recognized that whatever excellence it had was "rather rhetorical than poetical" (*Poems*, 69-73).

As the opposing armies prepared to break camp and to engage in battle, Timrod was moved to write one of his finest poems, "Spring." Kennedy Bryan has discerningly written that "Profoundly appealing as are Timrod's war strains, for they are the heart-cry of a people, still there is scarcely a battle-ode that does not close with an invocation to peace." Only at the end does "Spring" turn into a war poem; it may well be considered, in fact, as Timrod's most mature and most beautiful statement about nature. He presents an idyllic picture of a world ready to break into bloom, in a season that has a "nameless pathos in the air." Winter is ending; trees and flowers are turning green, although the turf is yet dark and new plants are just beginning to break through the earth. There is a "sense of blossoms yet unborn," a sense that spring is, or should be, a blessed and beneficent time. But the spring of 1863 will not be peaceful. The pathos will not be nameless. Abruptly, savagely, Timrod shifts from the idyllic to the tragic:

> Ah! who would couple thoughts of war and crime
> With such a blessed time!
> Who in the west wind's aromatic breath
> Could hear the call of Death!
>
> Yet not more surely shall the Spring awake
> The voice of wood and brake
> Than she shall rouse, for all her tranquil charms,
> A million men to arms.
>
> There shall be deeper hues upon her plains
> Than all her sunlit rains,
> And every gladdening influence around,
> Can summon from the ground.
>
> Oh! standing on this desecrated mould,
> Methinks that I behold,
> Lifting her bloody daisies up to God,
> Spring kneeling on the sod,
>
> And calling, with the voice of all her rills,
> Upon the ancient hills
> To fall and crush the tyrants and the slaves
> Who turn her meads to graves.

The poem is vibrantly emotional, but the emotion is restrained by the almost classic control of phrase and rhythm. Even the personification of spring as praying for peace seems to fit naturally, inevitably, into the context of the poem. [19]

Southern victories that spring lifted his spirits temporarily. But "Carmen Triumphale" is no undiluted song of triumph. Timrod bids "the land rejoice,/Yet not too gladly"; for when the sod is crimson, "intemperate glee is crime." There can, however, be a solemn satisfaction that the invaders have been driven back, that the foe has been soundly defeated, that "We need not heed their fangless wrath." Unfortunately, Timrod as a poet did not keep in mind the advice he gave to others. There is a renewed, vindictive anger against the Northern soldiers that led to intemperate statements and accusations; these weaken the poem instead of strengthening it. Momentarily at least, Timrod was again confident of victory; but the brightest hope was that it would speed the new nation "to the port of peace!" [20]

In several works Timrod had in a stanza or two paid incidental tribute to the bravery of Southern women. "The Two Armies" depicts their work and influence as being fully as valuable as that of the soldiers actually fighting; both are equally necessary if triumph is to be grasped, and freedom won (*Poems*, 158-60). He also paid tribute, in a better poem, to "The Unknown Dead." It is set in a framework: on a rainy night the poet hears the dull sound, similar to that when "the first spadeful drops like lead/Upon the coffin of the dead." This and the muffled church bell lead him to think of those who have been killed in Virginia, in the West, and along the Carolina coast. He is concerned not with the generals who have gained fame and are widely mourned, but with all the unidentified soldiers of whom it can only be said that "so many bravely fell." In a bitter conclusion, Timrod pictures them as mourned in individual homes, but as otherwise disregarded:

> And Nature's self, with eyes unwet,
> Oblivious of the crimson debt
> To which she owes her April grace,
> Laughs gayly o'er their burial-place.
> (*Poems*, 157-58)

Jay B. Hubbell has written me that he thinks "The Unknown Dead" is a "better poem than any of the numerous tributes to the Unknown Soldier of later wars."

In July, immediately after the attack on Fort Morris, Timrod again enlisted, but a hemorrhage on the same day abruptly and finally ended his military career. On July 23 he complained of being unemployed ("I have knocked at every door in vain"); but one knock evidently succeeded. Less than a month later, he was an assistant editor on the Charleston *Mercury*, for on August 12 he wrote to Rachel Lyons that his spirits had risen and his health had improved as a result of employment, even though the pay was too small for him to plan marriage and the reportorial task was hardly suited to his "tastes and habits." Worse, he soon found that steady work on a daily newspaper, where his job was to collect facts and reduce them to publishable form, was not conducive to writing: "the nervous state in which I am kept by the necessity I am under of being always on the *qui vive* for the last items is utterly incompatible with poetical achievement." He could produce nothing "except some occasional trifles."[21]

In January, 1864, he moved to Columbia, as part owner and associate editor of the *Daily South Carolinian.* He preferred writing editorials to working as a reporter and he could now afford to get married, but his opportunities for verse-writing were not improved. Simms, on a visit, noted that "his muse becomes costive and complains of his *mésalliances.*" True, the new editor had immediately published the most vigorous of his war sonnets, beginning "We may not falter, while there is an ell/Of ground on which to strike a foeman dead." It may have been written earlier, for Timrod wrote on August 25 to Hayne: "I have not written a line of verse for a twelve-month. All the poetry in my Nature has been fagged out of me I fear."

Timrod may have overstated slightly. He published less than a month later in the *South Carolinian* (September 21, 1864) an anonymous sonnet that is almost undoubtedly his own work. Angered by gossip about himself and even more by slander about his wife, Timrod opens with the bitter lines, "Soon must I leave this tongue-envenomed town/Where scandal holds her viper hissing court." In September he also wrote a short, delicate hymn to be sung at a sacred concert, asking that God hear "our cries for peace." But he was right in thinking that his poetic gifts were dormant.[22]

IV *Poems of Tragedy*

He had a magnificent if brief spurt of poetic energy in 1866. He was invited to write an ode to be sung at the Confederate Memorial exercises in Magnolia Cemetery in Charleston. The poem was sung on June 16 and printed in the *Courier* two days later, where it was described as "beautiful and soul-stirring, written by our native and gifted poet, HENRY TIMROD, which was sung most sweetly by the choir." It is his best poem, and probably his most popular one. The structure is classically simple. The "Ode" has the artistic merit of throbbing with vibrant emo-

tion in its effect upon a reader, yet of possessing a classic cool-
ness of phrase which might have been carved from stone. There
is no artistic exhibitionism; the verses are controlled and seem
inevitable.

But Timrod, an inveterate revisionist, was not satisfied. On
July 23, 1866, the *Courier* published "by request the amended
copy of the ode written by Mr. Timrod." The request no doubt
was made by the poet himself. He simplified the punctuation,
made several significant verbal changes, and rewrote the third
stanza. Since this revised version has rarely been reprinted (the
Hayne and Memorial editions reprint the June text), I give it
here:

I

Sleep sweetly in your humble graves,
Sleep, martyrs of a fallen cause!—
Though yet no marble column craves
The pilgrim here to pause.

II

In seeds of laurels in the earth
The garlands of your fame are sown;
And, somewhere, waiting for its birth,
The shaft is in the stone.

III

Meanwhile, your sisters for the years
Which hold in trust your storied tombs,
Bring all they now can give you—tears,
And these memorial blooms.

IV

Small tributes, but your shades will smile
As proudly on those wreaths today,
As when some cannon-moulded pile
Shall overlook this Bay.

V

Stoop angels hither from the skies!
There is no holier spot of ground
Than where defeated valor lies
By mourning beauty crowned.[23]

That year he also published three poems in *Scott's Monthly Magazine*. One editor had met Timrod: "He seemed to us the impersonation of a gentleness that won our heart at the first interview. Although reticent on other topics, we found him ready to communicate on the prospects of Southern literature. He expressed his cordial sympathy with this enterprise, then in its infancy, and promised to cooperate as he had leisure from other pressing engagements. Three of his latest and best productions have graced the pages of this magazine." The first, "The Rosebuds," may have been newly written, but it has the tone of his 1860-62 love poems. In any case, it is inconsequential.[24]

The other two, among his most poignant and pathetic works, grew out of memories of his dead son. "Our Willie" is an elegy and a remembrance. The poet remembers the Christmas Eve of 1864 when his child was born and brought such "mortal bliss" that the family forgot the sacredness of the time. The next Christmas there was no joy: "we kept/A mournful Christmas by the mound/Where little Willie slept." He turns back to the great joy that the baby had given them, until "that blue October night" when Willie died. Such grief cannot adequately be expressed: all that can be said is in "the brief 'Here lieth' of the dead!" This poem is too nakedly autobiographical a wail of agony to be read comfortably.

The companion piece, written for Katie rather than for Willie, is, on the contrary, one of his more complex pieces. As the title indicates, "A Mother's Wail" is a picture of grief, with the mother speaking throughout. To give richness to the poem, Timrod goes back to his earlier and long-neglected concept of dreams. In this poem the confusion of the senses, the inability to distinguish between dream and reality, is an artistic and dramatic device. The narrator sees in her mind three visions of her dead child: the baby himself, the mound of earth, and the cherub face in heaven. The dream-reality concept is essential to the structure of the poem: it works on a complex level to reveal the mother's emotions without reducing them to the indignity of a public outcry against fate. It is not surprising that John R. Thompson wrote to Hayne: "How magnificent was his 'Mother's Wail'! When I read his poems, I feel so deep a sense of utter inferiority that I almost vow I will never write another line." [25]

After that, Timrod was to write only a few unimportant poems. A sonnet published in *Scott's* seems to hint at forebodings of death: after describing the promise that life holds out and the beauties of nature, he concludes that, through these, God "in this mystic mode, would fain/Hint of a happier home, far, far away." Stimulated by his visit to "Copse Hill" in August, 1867, he wrote a little poem and sold it to *Southern Opinion* for a badly needed six dollars. A few trifles written on the flyleaves of albums or in scrapbooks have been ferreted out, but these—little better than such improvisations commonly are—certainly add nothing to his reputation.[26]

Shortly before his death he was again attempting to revise the proofsheets of his poems for a possible collected edition, but the most valuable revisions were made earlier, before the sheets were printed. Practically on his deathbed he wrote an obituary sonnet for Harris Simons; possibly because he felt that he could not take money derived from writing about a dead friend, the improvident Timrod cautioned Hayne: "You must not send it to Pollard, as I have given it away." This sonnet is neatly done, but it merely expresses the conventional sentiment that, although he will be sorely missed on earth, he will be happier in heaven, "To which thou shalt hereafter welcome us." Reading these lines, Hayne commented, "no shadow of a presentiment oppressed me. I simply admired the art of the Sonnet, and its tender Christian feeling, unconscious that another 'In Memoriam' would soon be called for."[27] This sonnet was undoubtedly Timrod's last poem.

CHAPTER 5

A Summing Up

I *Tributes*

AFTER TIMROD'S DEATH, his friends and admirers concentrated on two memorials: a collected edition of his
poetry, and an appropriate "memorial stone upon the grave of
the poet." Proceedings were not always amicable. William A.
Courtenay had promised Timrod that he would get out an edition of the poems, and he wished to do so. Paul Hamilton Hayne
felt that he should write the memoir of his closest friend, and
he appealed to the Timrod family. Courtenay claimed in 1898
that "I found the publisher in 1872, and Judge Bryan was to
write the memoir and edit the poems. How Mr. Hayne came into
it, I never understood." Perhaps memory betrayed him, for in
November, 1867, Emily Timrod Goodwin adjudicated the dispute by declaring roundly that she would not "pause for one
moment" between Hayne and Bryan, or any other man on earth:
"No one but Hal's dearest friend shall write Hal's biography." [1]

Hayne's *Memoir* is both generous and just. He freely admitted
Timrod's superiority to himself as a poet, at a time when his
own work had not been collected. His editing of the poems
was scrupulous, if not quite impeccable. He based most of his
text on the revised proofsheets that included a total of thirtynine poems, and most of the deviations seem to be typographical errors rather than editorial changes. Sixteen poems not
included in the proofsheets are taken verbatim from the 1859
Poems. For the remainder, Hayne used clippings or manuscripts,
and he seems to have followed them accurately. The same praise
cannot be accorded to his handling of the letters. Hayne's
changes are not extensive, but at times he made Timrod's plain

prose conform to his own more ornate style, and he sometimes overemphasized the pathos. This does not seem to be deliberate distortion, but rather a heightening for effect.[2]

Hayne worked under severe handicaps. He was at "Copse Hill," therefore removed from most of his source material; and he was too poverty-stricken to make extensive visits to Charleston and Columbia. A goodly part of his *Memoir* was written out of memory, and Hayne's memory was often treacherous. Too often, he was forced to depend upon the family for information and material: as an obvious example, the three editorials in the *Memoir* were sent to him at the last minute by Katie Timrod—and she made it quite clear that she had selected three that would not offend Northern readers. Hayne also made several errors of fact which later commentators have perpetuated, besides frequently adding one or two of their own. The defects in the Hayne edition are obvious. But it has many positive merits. The *Memoir* which Hayne called "simple" is in reality a warm-hearted yet discerning tribute to a friend and fellow poet: even when irritated by trying to straighten out some of its errors and generalizations, I find that I am still moved by it. Hayne was by no criterion a great writer, but he was a noble person.[3]

Apparently the book achieved all that Hayne had hoped for, and perhaps more. A second, enlarged edition appeared a few months later. The reviews were almost invariably favorable. If they dwelt more on the pathos of Timrod's life than on the nature and quality of his poetry, they at least called attention to his work. A typical one of these—and the one that Hayne valued most highly—was by Richard Henry Stoddard in the *Aldine*, April, 1873. It is lengthy, but in the main it retells from Hayne's *Memoir* the story of Timrod's tragic life—and Stoddard buttressed this story in order to reveal the "strait to which Timrod was reduced," by a long excerpt from the 1865 letters to him from Timrod. Hayne seems to have valued even more the sympathetic letters from John Greenleaf Whittier, praising the work of the dead poet.

One commentary that troubled and disconcerted Hayne was but indirectly related to his edition of Timrod's poems. More than a year after the publication of the second edition of Sidney Lanier's *Florida* (1876), Hayne wrote to his friendly fellow poet that "I have a small and not particularly black crow to pick with you." The offending passage had just caught his attention. Lanier had written that Timrod was one of the sweetest names connected with Charleston: "Few more spontaneous or delicate songs have been sung in these later days than one or two of the briefer lyrics which appear in the published volumes of his poems. It is thoroughly evident from these that he had never had time to learn the mere craft of the poet—the technique of verse. . . . But he had a dainty artless art withal." To prove this, Lanier quoted "Baby's Age," certainly one of Timrod's less important poems.

With reason heightened by irritation, Hayne attacked the idea that Timrod was ignorant of prosody and versification. Lanier was alone in thinking that Timrod sang his "native woodnotes wild"; all the "critiques, English and American," had agreed on "the singular delicacy and finish of T's verification; the unpretentious but *exquisite art which conceals itself.* . . . I have heard Timrod, for hours, discuss with scholars of the 'first water,' such men as Prof. Gildersleeve, formerly of *Göttingen,* now of the U. of Virginia,—the *profoundest* questions associated with both English and Latin prosody; displaying a subtle and minute acquaintance with his subject, which surprised those with whom he conversed. Excepting *Edgar Poe,* I don't believe the Southerner, nay, the American has ever existed, whose knowledge of the 'technique of verse' surpassed Timrod's." [4]

The group interested in erecting a memorial stone found the going slower even than Hayne had found it. A committee of distinguished older men set about this task. The roster was impressive: Hugh S. Thompson, State Superintendent of Education and later Governor; Federal Judge George S. Bryan; F. A. Porcher, President of the South Carolina Historical Society; James H. Carlyle, President of Wofford College; and Ellison Capers, Episcopalian rector in Greenville, recently a brigadier-general in the Confederate army and later Bishop of South Carolina. The results were less impressive. William James Rivers, Timrod's onetime teacher, gave a lecture on the characteristics of Timrod's poetry; this was published under the cumbersome but explicit title, *A Little Book: to Obtain Means for Placing a Memorial Stone upon the Grave of the Poet Henry Timrod.* Friends were asked to pay from two to five dollars a copy, but the book sold slowly: "The responses were not such as I had hoped for, and when the cost of publication had been paid, I had not quite $90 for the monument," wrote Hugh Thompson, treasurer of the committee. This was sufficient for a "plain shaft of polished white Italian marble eight and a half feet in height, resting on a base of Winnsboro granite." On three sides there were quotations from Timrod's poems; on one, the statement "Erected by the Poet's Friends." [5]

There were various, published literary tributes. Simms immediately wrote a laudatory article, "The Late Henry Timrod," for *Southern Society.* Easily the most discerning lecture was the one by John Dickson Bruns, Timrod's longtime friend and onetime schoolmate. There were poetic tributes by the Northern writer Henry Austin and by Carl McKinley; the best elegy, fittingly enough, was Hayne's "At the Grave of Henry Timrod"—although Dr. Wauchope seems over-generous in his praise when he called it "the most deeply touching elegy in our literature." [6]

What is frequently known as the "Timrod Revival" began in 1899. Hayne was dead and his edition long out of print. William A. Courtenay that year organized The Timrod Memorial Association, with the dual purpose of bringing out a collected edition of Timrod's poems and of erecting suitable monuments to his memory. Courtenay succeeded with both projects. The Memorial Edition appeared in 1899, under the Houghton Mifflin imprint but with a subscription guarantee by the Association. The text is in the main reliable. Of the eighty-two poems included, seventy-three are taken directly from Hayne's text. Another, Timrod's last poem, "In Memoriam—Harris Simons," was taken from Hayne's *Memoir* and transferred to last place among the sonnets. Two others, listed in a final section under the title "Poems now first collected," had appeared in the 1859 edition, although one had been greatly revised, and the Memorial Edition followed Hayne in omitting three poems from the earlier book. The defects in the new work are obvious. Cardwell's stricture is so accurately phrased that I quote it: "The editing was casual, the arrangement of the poems is awkward and inaccurate, and the introduction by J. P. Kennedy Bryan adds little to our knowledge of the poet."

Financially the work was a success. Four thousand copies were sold, more because of the personal efforts and appeals of Courtenay than of any active campaign by the publisher. The Association erected in Washington Square, Charleston, a bronze bust of Timrod, made by the sculptor Edward Valentine; it was set on a shaft of granite. The monument in Columbia was replaced by a granite boulder. It is perhaps ironical that the greatest service to Timrod's memory was that Courtenay had the Timrod manuscripts bound along with the records and letters of the Association's work, and then deposited them in the Charleston Library Society. As a final achievement, he sold the copyright, plates, and some two hundred copies of unbound sheets to the B. F. Johnson Publishing Company, of Richmond, for one thousand dollars. This money he sent to Henry Timrod's widow, Kate Timrod Lloyd.[7]

This activity led to many local and to a few national articles, most notably by Henry Austin and Hamilton Wright Mabie. They are laudatory and in some instances discerning; unfortunately, none was based on fresh research, with the result that many errors were repeated. By far the best of these critical revaluations did not appear until 1903, after the slight furor had become practically quiescent. Ludwig Lewisohn then compared the texts of the sonnets in the 1859 and in the Hayne editions; the revisions, he concluded, reveal a "craftsman whose artistic conscience is no less sensitive than his moral conscience."[8] Possibly the finest tribute, undoubtedly inspired by the Memorial Edition, was Lizette Woodworth Reese's excellent sonnet, "Timrod," published in the *Atlantic Monthly,* January, 1900.

Except for a few competent scholarly articles, especially those by G. P. Voigt and Guy Cardwell, little was written about Timrod until the early 1940's. Jay B. Hubbell in 1941 brought out his excellent study, *The Last Years of Henry Timrod,* with many letters from and about him, drawn mainly from the Duke Collection. The following year Guy A. Cardwell published and carefully edited all of Timrod's known early verse, and he wrote a valuable introduction; shortly afterward, and issued as a companion volume, appeared my edition of *The Essays of Henry Timrod.* But this work represents, at most, half the task that needs doing. Although some letters have been published in small magazines, there is no well-annotated collected edition of the letters; although the text of the Memorial Edition is a good one, the poems need to be more attractively presented and to be arranged in some logical order (preferably chronologically, insofar as that can be determined). Above all, there is no good or even reliable biography. As Hubbell has noted, "the comparative neglect of Timrod in our literary history was not, as his Southern admirers often maintained, an antipathy to the Confederate poet but simply the lack of adequate sources of information about the man and his work." [9]

II   *Reputation*

It would be an act of critical folly to claim that Timrod was a major poet or critic, even among nineteenth-century American writers. Clearly he was not. He did not have the germinal force or the international influence of a Poe or a Whitman; he lacked the tough and roughened originality of Emerson. Neither will his work awaken the belated excitement that Emily Dickinson's has justifiably aroused. He was a conventional writer in poetic forms and, before the Civil War, in ideas. Yet in his own time he failed notably to achieve the kind of reputation that Longfellow, Whittier, Lowell, and later Lanier—poets with whom he can properly be compared—did manage to achieve.

In part, he was born too late. He was a belated Romantic, though markedly less so than his friend Hayne. A follower of Wordsworth and Tennyson, Timrod had in his early poems only a little to add to what the greater English poets had written about nature. That little grew out of his own darker spirit. The element of doubt and of questioning gives a fascinating if fleeting richness, complexity, and originality to his work, especially when he ties nature in with his more modern concept of dreams.

Less can be said for the love poems. Alone among critics, William Dean Howells preferred them to the war lyrics; he considered Timrod's genius to be "essentially meditative and tenderly lyrical." [10] Of the early poems of this kind, "Praeceptor Amat" is strikingly clever, and well sustains a half-gallant, half-sentimental attitude with a gloss of playfulness. But Timrod was rarely interested in the detached if sincere gallantry of the Cavalier poets. Too often the pretty faces that acted on him as a poetic catalyst led him to personal sentimentality rather than to objectified sentiment. This is not always true of the later poems: "Katie" and "La Belle Juive" have enough artistry as well as feeling to be read with pleasure today. Yet no one of these has the skillful use of metaphor, the depth of thought and imagery, and the power that characterize and individualize his elegiac "A Mother's Wail."

Only two of his editorials and critical essays have continuing importance, and one of these, "Literature in the South," has that primarily as a part of American intellectual history. His objections to Southernism or nationalism are a necessarily integral component in the works of American writers. He pleaded for less prejudice in region and nation, yet at the same time for more independence of judgment. This involved changing outmoded standards of literary values; it also involved a fair judging of what had been achieved. Of Southern writers, only Poe "has received his full measure of fame. The immense resources and versatile powers of Simms are to this day grudgingly acknowledged, or contemptuously denied." A fair recognition did not entail exalting mediocrity; instead Timrod advocated no puffing, no "quarter for the dunce." But writers like Simms were too often "alluded to with contempt by individuals who had never read anything beyond the title-pages of his books." He did not believe that originality or nationality depended upon subject matter; indeed, true originality, regardless of the locale of the work, would always be "found identical with true nationality." Before the country can have great writing, it must have a reformation in taste; for it "is, unfortunately, not in the power of a people to confer together and say, 'Come, now, let us arise and build up a literature'" (*Essays*, 96-97).

"A Theory of Poetry" has considerable importance in itself. Timrod dismisses briefly William J. Grayson's attempt to define poetry simply as verse, whether good or bad, apparently feeling that this definition had been demolished in his earlier essay, "What is Poetry?". He was more disturbed by Poe's contention that only the brief subjective lyric can be true poetry. This seemed unduly to narrow the scope and the matter of poetry. Fine poems could be written with beauty as the ultimate, the only, aim of the poet. Both Poe and Tennyson had demonstrated that this could be done. But their works of this kind were not among the greatest poems. For this, two other qualities were needed: power and truth. The finest poets were always ethical poets.

Poe was likewise wrong in trying to restrict the scope, by ruling out the epic as a legitimate form. Using *Paradise Lost,* Timrod attempted to prove that an epic can have artistic unity and ethical content—and to its enrichment rather than to its detriment. Moreover, Poe was psychologically wrong in his belief that a poem must be read at one sitting, in order that a psychic excitement be maintained. There is another, equally valid way of reading. The thoughtful reader as he begins, say, the third book of *Paradise Lost* will bring "with him all the impressions of his former reading to heighten the colour and deepen the effect of that which is before him." This type of reader is not content to pass through "a series of transient though noble excitements"; when he finishes *Paradise Lost,* his mind is filled with "a long train of lofty thought and unsurpassable imagery." The essay is an effective defense of ethical poetry as exemplified in the work of Milton and of Wordsworth, and is the only good refutation of Poe's argument that I have seen. It has lost neither its value nor its validity (*Essays,* 108-11).

In spite of some excellent work in criticism and in other kinds of poetry, Timrod seems destined to be known, as H. T. Thompson called him, as "the Laureate of the Confederacy." This is not an ignominious title, but it is a limiting one. Partially it is misleading, and to that extent it has done harm to his reputation and to his work. His best poems are not Confederate poems: they are a protest against the horror of war. Yet there is, of course, some justification for the title. In its beginning, the new nation and the war gave Timrod a theme. It matured his poetic talents. In "A Vision of Poesy" he had declared that "the poet to the whole wide world belongs," but the world was forgotten in his intense, narrowed absorption with something which lay nearer his hand and his heart.

Before the war, he had mastered a technique, without really having much to say. Now this technical mastery and his intellectual turn of mind served him well: although throbbing emotion beats through his words in passionate undertones, the passion never carries the verse into formlessness of thought or reference. It is this quality that sets Timrod's early war poetry apart from many similarly patriotic poems, that gives it a quality of memorable distinction. "Ethnogenesis" and "The Cotton Boll" are stately and readable odes: "Carolina" and "A Cry to Arms" are inspiriting appeals to a people to defend their rights and their land. These are his best in this vein, but Timrod wrote others. If he had written nothing else, Thompson's subtitle would be accurate.

Yet these are not Timrod's best poems. It is, rather, when he uses war as a terrifying background that Timrod approaches poetic greatness. His city, Charleston, is with calm assurance awaiting certain attack; she may be destroyed, but her citizens will not dishonor her history and her traditions. Christmas brings with it a desire not so much for victory as simply for peace— "peace in all our hearts." As early as December, 1861, Timrod wondered "whether this damnable war will ever end." [11] After his experience as war correspondent, he was never unaware of war's horror. Even Southern victories were lauded only because they might hasten the coming of peace. Spring, which once brought an indefinable ecstasy to man's spirit, now brought also the inescapable awareness of imminent bloodshed.

These are not, in the strict sense, martial poems. They are against war. They are an appeal not to arms but to peace. They represent Timrod at his best, humanly and poetically. It is appropriate, then, that his finest single poem should be a mournful celebration not of a dead nation but of the men who had died for it. There is a significant difference. In a good poem, Timrod had hymned the birth of a new nation; in his best poem, he wrote only of the dead.

Notes and References

Chapter One

1. G. S. Gongaware, *The History of the German Friendly Society* (Richmond, 1935), pp. 7-11. On January 19, 1774 (and earlier), he is consistently listed as Henry Dimrod, Vice-President; on January 26, as Henry Timrod, President. After that, he remained Timrod. His marriage was listed in *Gazette of the State of South-Carolina*, March 24, 1785. The *Gazette*, May 4, 1765, lists him as a shoemaker. The best general article on the poet's ancestry is ex-mayor John F. Ficken's "Timrod's Ancestry," in *Proceedings of the Timrod Memorial Association.*

2. Paul Hamilton Hayne, *The Poems of Henry Timrod*, pp. 8-9 (hereafter cited as Hayne); letter, Emily Timrod Goodwin to Paul Hamilton Hayne, December 2, 1867, in the Hayne Collection, Duke University Library.

3. Letter quoted in Hayne, 10n. The wording of a posthumous tribute (Charleston *Evening News*, March 28, 1848) sounds like Bryan:

> The following verses of our deceased townsman Wm. H. Timrod are for the first time published. All who remember the pleasant man, so genial and so gentle, and have enjoyed the effusions of his gentle muse will be glad to receive anything which will remind them of the friend so much loved, and the poet so much admired. South Carolina has many names of which she has a right to be proud, and many *prouder* names than that of the humble author of these lines. But the name of Timrod should be dear to her. In spite of every thing in his lot to crush a generous spirit—born to poverty—denied education—struggling with misfortune all his days, and nailed down to the *work-bench*—he has yet left behind him thought and sentiment, clothed in language which none of her sons, however gifted or educated, have surpassed. . . .

4. Hayne, 41n; Ficken, "Timrod's Ancestry." John Rudolph Faesch was a native of Switzerland who emigrated to this country before 1775. But it was through Hannah Caesar that the age-old rumor started that Timrod was of Negro blood. Although without foundation in fact, the rumor had some justification. After Hannah Caesar had been robbed, her testimony was challenged in court by Gen. C. C. Pinckney, attorney for the defendants, on the ground that

she was of mixed blood. This challenge was quickly dropped, and was not mentioned in the appeal after the defendants were convicted. Apparently Pinckney had confused two quite different cases. In 1754 a Dr. Cesar, "Practitioner of Physick," had left the residue of his property "for the benefit of my daughter Hannah at this time slave to . . . John Norman." This tangled and confused record was first unravelled by Rupert Taylor, in "Henry Timrod's Ancestress, Hannah Caesar," *American Literature*, IX (January, 1938), pp. 419-30. According to Emily (Hayne, 41n.), William Henry Timrod liked and admired his father-in-law, describing him as "the most upright and honest man I ever knew."

5. See Guy A. Cardwell, Jr., "The Date of Henry Timrod's Birth," *American Literature*, VII (May, 1935), pp. 207-8. The date is given as 1829 on his tombstone and in most earlier books and articles, but William Henry Timrod's Daybook for 1825-29 (in the Charleston Library Society) proves that 1828 is correct. The name is given as Henry H. Timrod; Cardwell conjectures (rightly, I think) that the H. stood for Hagan, the maiden name of William's mother. That Hayne was uncertain about the date of birth is indicated by a letter to him from Emily Timrod Goodwin (MS in the South Caroliniana Library): "With regard to our brother's age I must be candid with you. The year of his birth was written down by my father as the 8th of December 1829; but Hal always said 1830. He thought he had accomplished so little that he made himself a year younger than he really was."

Rebecca was crippled. A niece of Thyrza Prince, who signed herself "Cousin Sallie," wrote to W. A. Courtenay that "Rebecca was a saint." Her father in 1828 wrote a poem for her which he preserved in his Daybook; it shows, as Herman Felder noted (p. 9), "more religious sentiment than parental affection":

> My daughter when you older grow
> And learn your limbs defects to know
> Grieve not that God hath formed you so.
> Haply your Maker hath designed
> Your limb imperfect that your mind
> May not be to yourself confined.

6. Daybook, 1825-29, in Charleston Library Society; Virginia Pettigrew Clare, *Harp of the South*, p. 27 (quoted from notes made for an unfinished sketch of Timrod's life by Mrs. Edith Goodwin Dearing). A newspaper clipping, dated September 9, 1828, and preserved in the Daybook, states that "William Henry Timrod is made director of the Franklin Library Society."

7. Hayne, p. 9. Simms included four of the poems in *The Charles-*

ton Book (1844); Hayne, five in his memoir. At least four fragments of the lost play were published: *Southern Literary Journal*, I (December, 1835), pp. 270-73; n.s. IV (October, 1838), pp. 311-16; n.s. IV (December, 1838), pp. 438-48; and *The Southern Rose*, V (August 5, 1837), p. 200. *The Southern Rose* also printed his "To Time" in the issue of Oct. 29, 1836, V, 40. I am indebted to Prof. Hubbell for this information.

The play is set in Renaissance Italy, and features a wealthy but grasping art collector and money-lender, Salviati. When he offered Cellini only half the sum that the artist demanded for a vase, Cellini put it on an anvil and shattered it with a hammer. Timrod illustrates various facets of Salviati's overweening pride. The play is in irregular but attractively written blank verse.

8. The clearest and best account is by Guy A. Cardwell, Jr.: "William Henry Timrod, the Charleston Volunteers, and the Defense of St. Augustine," *North Carolina Historical Review*, XVIII (January, 1941), pp. 27-37. See also Gongaware, *op. cit.* Timrod's manuscript account of the expedition is in the Charleston Library Society. In the 1837-38 *City Directory* he is listed both as Customs House Inspector and as a bookbinder at 10 Broad Street.

9. Herman M. Felder, "Notes on Timrod" (Unpublished Vanderbilt Thesis, 1936), pp. 11-12; Gongaware, *op. cit.*, pp. 44 ff.; MS records of the German Friendly Society.

10. G. E. Manigault, "The Classical School of Mr. Christopher Cotes," in Colyer Meriwether's *History of Higher Education in South Carolina* (Washington, 1899), pp. 30-37. Manigault indicates that Hayne at another school had become an excellent orator; on the rare occasions when that pastime was allowed, Hayne was sure of a good and enthusiastic audience. By contrast, Timrod was a diffident speaker, given to stuttering slightly when he was excited.

11. Hayne, p. 17, writing from memory many years later, seems to have confused Cotes, an Englishman, with his chief assistant, William E. Bailey. Cotes reserved chastisement for himself, but Hayne may have done him an injustice, as Cotes claimed that he had seen too many assistants lose their tempers while punishing the boys. Basil L. Gildersleeve in "Formative Influences," *Forum*, X (February, 1891), pp. 607-17, notes his unpleasant recollections of Bailey and characterizes him as "a severe drill master."

12. William J. Rivers, *A Little Book: To Obtain Means for Placing a Memorial Stone upon the Grave of the Poet Henry Timrod*, p. 8; Hayne, pp. 17-18.

13. John Dickson Bruns delivered this lecture at the Central Presbyterian Church in Charleston, October 27, 1870, and it was reported at length in the Charleston *Courier*, October 28. Judge George S.

Bryan, introducing the speaker, noted that he had "intimately known from earliest childhood" both the speaker and the dead poet, "our sweetest singer." The Charleston *News*, October 28, 1870, was less sympathetic: "If no vigorous criticism was attempted, none was desired, or perhaps none needed." This was niggardly, if not unfair; although Bruns makes it clear that he spoke as a close friend and admirer rather than as an unbiased commentator, he has many perceptive observations. I have used the complete text as printed in the Charleston *Sunday News*, April 30, 1899. It was also collected under the title, "Life and Genius of Timrod," in *Memories of the Timrod Revival*, 1898-1901 (Charleston Library Society).

14. Quoted in Hayne, pp. 41-42n. Emily's admiration for her mother was not half-hearted: "To this strong love of Nature, she added so correct a judgment in all things; so much sound practical sense; such self-abnegation and entire devotion to those she loved; and such sweetness, forbearance, gentleness, that I think I can truly say, she was one of the most perfect characters I ever knew!"

15. These early poems are in the manuscript collection, *Autographic Relics*, in the Charleston Library Society. Guy Cardwell has printed all these poems, with useful introduction and notes, in his *The Uncollected Poems of Henry Timrod* (Athens, Ga., 1942). On these, see pp. 3, 23, and 78.

16. Thompson, *Henry Timrod*, p. 15n. Felder, p. 14, suggests that this "might well have been inscribed somewhat enviously to the precocious Gildersleeve."

17. Thompson, p. 15. Bruns is more specific: Timrod "could not have worshipped at a purer shrine" than that of Wordsworth; as for Tennyson, the "laureate's intoxicating vintage" was so powerful that "all of our young men have drunken of that magician's wine." Bryan, p. xxxiii, states flatly, but without citing any authority, that Timrod reflected the elegance of Catullus, "always his delight, and a metrical translation of whose poems he had completed." This seems doubtful. Apparently no such manuscript has survived, and Kate Timrod Lloyd, in a letter to W. A. Courtenay, May 15 [1898], wrote that "I cannot recall that he commenced a metrical version of Catullus, but I have no doubt that he contemplated doing it at one time, but I am sure it was never begun." See also Cardwell, pp. 3-5; E. W. Parks, *The Essays of Henry Timrod* (Athens, Ga., 1942), pp. 34-56; and Hayne, p. 18.

18. E. W. Parks, "Timrod's College Days," *American Literature*, VIII (November, 1936), pp. 294-96. This article is based on the *Minutes of the Faculty of the University of Georgia* (unnumbered pages); on the *Catalogue of the Officers and Students of Franklin College, University of Georgia, 1844-1845;* the *Tuition Book of the*

University of Georgia, p. 157; and the *Minutes of the Demosthenian Society, 1840-1847* (unnumbered pages). Clare, *Harp of the South*, p. 30, writes that a Charleston merchant named Ross made it financially possible for Timrod to attend the University. This was probably James Ross, listed as merchant in the 1837-38 *City Directory* and as Port Warden in 1849. W. H. Timrod had worked in the Customs House.

19. Clare, p. 30; Hayne, p. 19. Both of these poems are in "Autographic Relics," and are reprinted by Cardwell, pp. 53-54 and 40 (with the title "Choice in Eyes" and with a few changes). Another poem from "Autographic Relics," with the first line, "We walk'd beneath the shadow," was published over the pseudonym "Aglaus" in the *Southern Literary Gazette*, II (Sept. 1, 1849), p. 18.

20. Cardwell, pp. 32, 55, 58. See also E. M. Coulter, *College Life in the Old South* (rev. ed.; Athens, Georgia, 1951), p. 212.

21. Hayne, pp. 21-22n. (quoting from a letter from Judge George S. Bryan).

22. Bruns, "A Lecture on Timrod," Charleston *Sunday News*, April 30, 1899.

23. William Gilmore Simms, "The Late Henry Timrod," *Southern Society*, I (Oct. 12, 1867), pp. 18-19; reprinted in Jay B. Hubbell, *The Last Years of Henry Timrod*, pp. 152-65. For Emily Goodwin's letter, see Hubbell, p. 86; on his welcome to Charleston, Hayne, p. 22. Bruns agreed with Simms that Timrod's muse was "singularly reticent" and that his "genius was meditative rather than passionate." On January 4, 1862, Timrod wrote to Emily that "Bruns made a remark which afforded me a great deal of pleasure. He says that it is my peculiar lot to have won, without wealth or power, a larger circle of strongly attached friends than any man of his acquaintance."

24. George A. Wauchope, *Henry Timrod: Man and Poet*, pp. 12, 15. John R. Thompson, editor of the *Southern Literary Messenger*, identified Aglaus as Timrod when in XXII (February, 1856), p. 89, Timrod signed the verses beginning "We met but once" with his own name. After that, his work is signed Henry Timrod. His friend Hayne was associate editor and then editor of the *Southern Literary Gazette* in 1852.

25. Yates Snowden, "A Reminiscence of Henry Timrod," Charleston *News and Courier*, December 20, 1903. Snowden lists as his authority an unidentified "kindred spirit" who was present and "furnished the details of this little story." Apparently Timrod recited better than he spoke. Wauchope, p. 13, notes that his "voice was a deep rich bass, very soft and musical." Hayne, p. 20, notes that he was fond of argument, but that he had not as an extemporaneous speaker, "inherited his father's faculty of language and illustration. . . .

On the other hand, he was an admirable reader, even if his style *did* sometimes verge on the theatrical." Hayne especially remembered Timrod in early manhood reciting Wordsworth's "Ode on Intimations of Immortality." A similar hoax was perpetrated on the Augusta poet, Richard Henry Wilde.

26. Paul Hamilton Hayne, "Ante-Bellum Charleston," *Southern Bivouac*, IV (October and November, 1885), pp. 257-68, 328-36, esp. 258 and 328-30; W. P. Trent, *William Gilmore Simms*, pp. 227-32.

27. E. W. Parks, *William Gilmore Simms as Literary Critic* (Athens, Ga., 1961), esp. pp. 89-93, 141. Timrod's only known translation from German poetry is "Song of Mignon," from Goethe's *Wilhelm Meister*. The MS is in the Ferris Collection, Columbia University Library; it is printed in Cardwell, pp. 103-4. Both Cardwell, p. 120, n. 91, and other writers, seem to have confused this translation with Timrod's poem, "1866. Addressed to the Old Year." It was the latter that was published in the *Daily South Carolinian*, December 31, 1866, and that Simms described as "not worthy of his pen" when he sent the MS copy to W. H. Hawkins on January 2, 1866. See Simms' *Letters*, IV, p. 531.

28. Based mainly on unpublished information furnished to me by Prof. Isaac Copeland of George Peabody College for Teachers. There is some useful information in Edgar Knight's *Documentary History of Education in the South before 1860* (5 vols. 1949-53), and in his earlier *Public Education in the South* (1821). I have also drawn on several of Timrod's letters to his sister Emily and to Rachel Lyons.

29. Thompson, p. 19; Wauchope, pp. 14-15. Thompson mistakenly says that Timrod's first job was in the school at Bluffton, S. C. He did not go there until May, 1860, after approximately ten years of tutoring. Lowndes was a not uncommon name in South Carolina. I have not been able to identify this particular man or plantation.

30. Letters to his sister Emily, July 4, 1851; October 3, 1851; July 29, 1853; in the South Caroliniana Library. The third letter is headed as from "The Meadows," the name of Blake's home near Fletcher, North Carolina. In the first letter he complained of an eruption on the skin "exactly like the one Rebecca had," and asked what she had done for it. He wouldn't write directly to her because "in the present state of her health, I don't wish to subject her to the toil of writing." As an afterthought, he tacked on at the end that there was no Fourth of July celebration, and that Mrs. Blake "a week ago, blest her Lord with an addition to his family."

31. Wauchope, pp. 12-13, who quotes from a letter written to him by Felicia Robinson. From Orangeburg on April 10, 1856, Timrod

wrote an appreciative letter to Oscar Keeler, a Northern admirer of his early poems; it is printed in "Some Letters of Henry Timrod," with a foreword by Thomas Ollive Mabbott, in *The American Collector*, III (February, 1927), pp. 191-95. Timrod expressed surprise at his name's being known, since as a writer his name was yet "so obscure." Simms, a frequent translator himself, testified in "The Late Henry Timrod" (Hubbell, p. 157) that Timrod was "a good Latin scholar, something of a Grecian, and possessed a fair general acquaintance with some of the Continental languages." Timrod frequently revisited the Robinson plantation; in a letter to Emily from Hardeeville, March 12, 1861, he writes that he will probably stop at Murray Robinson's on his way to Columbia.

32. Thompson, pp. 21-22; Clare, p. 43. Thompson adds that during the war Timrod "refugeed for a time at 'Forest Cottage'." The tiny school building which is now the Timrod Museum is of interest mainly as showing the ordinary, inexpensive plantation school, as contrasted with the elaborate ones on several plantations in Virginia. Few of Timrod's books there have any annotations; they are primarily of sentimental or associational value. There is a three-volume set of Bacon and an eight-volume set of Milton. Since Timrod lived with the Goodwins and not with the Cannon family, he received $1,000 a year instead of his customary stipend of $800.

33. Hayne, *op. cit.*; *Southern Bivouac*, IV (November, 1885), p. 330; Trent, pp. 229-31.

34. Thompson, p. 23. See Hayne, above.

35. Hayne in later life made a curious but consistent error about *Russell's:* he speaks of it as living for two years and filling four volumes (see *Southern Bivouac*, IV, 330). Hayne, *Memoir*, p. 24, noted that in "The Arctic Voyager" he had detected "for the first time in our author's art, the influence of Tennyson, not superseding, but harmoniously blending with the earlier influence of Wordsworth."

36. *Russell's Magazine*, I (May, 1857), pp. 156-59; reprinted in *The Essays of Henry Timrod*, pp. 61-68.

37. *Russell's*, I (July, 1857), pp. 327-37. This is Grayson's article. Timrod's answer appeared in *Russell's*, II (October, 1857), pp. 52-58. Both are reprinted in *The Essays of Henry Timrod*. A. S. Salley, in his fragmentary Timrod bibliography in *Southern Historical Association Publications*, III (October, 1899), pp. 274-80, attributed both articles to Timrod; he has been uncritically followed, or the same error has been made, by Clare and various others. In his manuscript autobiography (South Caroliniana Library; quoted in *Essays*, p. 174), Grayson drily remarks that he had once charged Wordsworth with being mechanical in his response to nature and "was nearly anni-

hilated by an indignant admirer [Timrod] who overwhelmed me with quotations to prove how much I was in error. The quotations did not change my opinions."

38. *Russell's*, (August, 1859), pp. 385-95; reprinted in *The Essays of Henry Timrod*. In the *Courant*, I (May 4, 1859), p. 1, a magazine published at Columbia, H. H. Caldwell wrote: "We see in the Cheraw papers accounts of the Lecture of Henry Timrod, our young Carolina Petrarch, who has been holding forth on 'The Southern Author'."

39. Hayne, pp. 29-30; Cardwell, pp. 8-9. The book was copyrighted 1859, but on the title page the date is 1860. These dates have been used interchangeably to refer to the same edition. Bruns consistently referred to the 1859 *Poems*, Hayne to 1860. A note in the Charleston *Courier*, December 22, 1859, indicates that 1859 is preferable: "*Timrod's Poems*—At an hour too late for anything beyond a brief acknowledgment, we have received the long-expected volume of 'Poems by Henry Timrod' issued by Ticknor and Fields, Boston." Perhaps with the hope of getting a place in the University of South Carolina, he called in Columbia soon afterward on Augustus Baldwin Longstreet, president of the college and well-known author of *Georgia Scenes*. A student has described the visit, in February, 1860: "we all sat down and the old Judge got out his pipe and fell to smoking, and we all chatted together until the arrival of another guest. This was Mr. Timrod, the young Charleston poet, quite a nice looking, but a very little man. During the conversation he spoke of a peculiarly sweet and plaintive Indian air, which he had heard that the Judge played, whereupon that gentleman very obligingly got up and fetched his flute (an elegant glass one), and played the air. It was really beautiful." (Edward L. Green, *History of the University of South Carolina*, Columbia, S. C., 1916, p. 358.) But no offer was forthcoming.

40. Letter to Emily, May 8, 1860; in South Caroliniana Library. Wauchope, p. 14, gives the name correctly as Train, but Thompson, pp. 18-19, for some reason changed it to Fenn, although he cites Wauchope as his source. I have also seen the name transcribed as Levin. But an examination of Timrod's letter by me and by several qualified people in the South Caroliniana Library revealed that the name was undoubtedly Train.

41. Wauchope, pp. 13-14. Wauchope gives no source, but is circumstantially convincing. He notes that Train's left arm "on account of some stiffness in his shoulder-joint, stood out as rigid as a bar of iron," and that the culprit "suddenly felt himself in the clutches of that terrible, derrick-like arm."

42. Letters to Emily, June 11, 1860, and January 29, 1861; in

South Caroliniana Library. Any improvement in health was at best temporary. In 1901 a doctor who signed himself J. H. M. [Mellichampe] wrote from New Orleans to his brother Robert E. Mellichampe of Charleston that he had known Timrod in Bluffton and had "even attended him when he was sick and suffering." The writer added that reading the Memorial Edition of Timrod's poems brought tears to his eyes, and he was also grateful for several articles that showed a "just appreciation of my old friend."

43. The date of moving from Charleston to Columbia is given in a letter from Emily to Hayne, Washington, August 4, 1872. Mr. and Mrs. Goodwin, their four children, and Katie moved; Mrs. W. H. Timrod, Rebecca, and Edyth stayed in Charleston. The definitive article on this love affair is M. B. Siegler's "Henry Timrod and Sophie Sosnowski," *Georgia Historical Quarterly*, XXXI (September, 1947), pp. 172-80. Timrod's letters are in the South Caroliniana Library. On May 8, 1860, Timrod sent through Emily "My love, if she is not afraid of its burning her; and tell her that her tress of hair—though it was stolen—has already saved me from a great temptation." But on June 18 he wrote that her passions were "no stronger than water and moonlight." He compared the strength of his feelings with the strength of the albatross, but which could be completely disabled by a sudden rain: "This incapacity the bird owes to the size and power of the wings which bear it so grandly from continent to continent, but which at the same time in the event of a tempest, absorb a greater amount of moisture, and retain it for a longer period, than the plumage of smaller birds." A year later (June 11, 1861), he did not wish her to be mortified by his words or actions: "I love her no longer indeed, but I still feel toward her tenderly enough to wish to save her from the slightest mortification. I shall certainly write to her and tell her that though she is not the Miss Sophie of my imagination, she is still a very lovable little person, and I shall be glad to have her dearest friendship."

44. For the poem, see Cardwell, pp. 95-96. Timrod's letters to Rachel Lyons have been edited by William Fidler and published in the *Southern Literary Messenger*, II (October, November, December, 1940), pp. 527-35, 605-11, 645-51; and in the *Alabama Review*, II (April, 1949), pp. 139-49. On June 11, 1861, Timrod wrote to Emily that he "received last week a very pleasant letter from Miss Rachel Lyons. She is rapidly conquering my old prejudice against the Hebrew."

45. Letters to Emily, March 12, 1861, and June 11, 1861. In the first letter, Timrod notes that "one of these days I may correct my ode for a second volume," and expressed pleasure at the praise of "Ethnogenesis": "I am rejoiced to hear that Miss Sophie is pleased

with my ode. Hayne has written me to say that there is but one opinion among all my friends in regard to the 'great merit' of the piece. Simms has also sent me his congratulations." Scrawled across the top of the letter: "My toothache is better, but my face is ludicrously swollen." He was pleased that Emily's children were in school, as this would save Rebecca the worry of teaching them.

46. See note 45. A copy of the broadside is in the Harris Collection, John Hay Library, Brown University, titled "Ode on the Meeting of the Southern Congress. By H. Timrod." The projected poem on an Arctic voyage was clearly meant to be a longer, more ambitious, and presumably quite different poem from his "Arctic Voyager," already published in *Russell's*, April, 1857, and in the 1859 *Poems*. The quotations from his letters are in the *Southern Literary Messenger*, II (1940), pp. 534-35, 607-9, and 645-46.

47. *Southern Literary Messenger*, II, pp. 646-48; Hubbell, p. 11. In a letter to Emily, February 21, 1862, Timrod wrote that in order to get an outfit he had "been constrained much against my will to enroll myself as a private (enlisted for twelve months) in the Orangeburg Company from which Keitt details me as his secretary." But a carriage in which he was riding had overturned, and his side was so painfully injured that he could not immediately enter upon his duties.

48. Keitt had given Timrod a three-month leave of absence: S L M, II, p. 650. Hayne, p. 42; Bruns, "A Lecture on Timrod." Randall's letter is quoted in Hubbell, pp. 12-13. "Personne" was the pen-name of Felix Gregory De Fontaine, later Timrod's associate on the *Daily South Carolinian*, and already a noted war correspondent.

49. Letters to Rachel Lyons, July 25, and October 28, 1862, in *Alabama Review*, II (April, 1949), pp. 139-49. In the first letter he enclosed two poems inspired by Katie Goodwin, with the caution: "Don't let my extravagance do Katie an injury with you. Remember that a poet has the right to idealize, and a lover to be hyperbolical." For Timrod's trenchant remarks on the war, see his letters in the South Caroliniana Library.

50. Cardwell, pp. 11-16; Hayne, p. 40; Hubbell, pp. 34n., 40, 43. As Hubbell notes, Hayne intensified the plaintive tone by changing a few words: "'An unspeakable disappointment! but I try to bear my lot—the lot' he adds, with a momentary bitterness, 'of all impecunious poets.'"

51. Letter to Rachel Lyons, July 23, 1863, S L M, II (December, 1940), p. 650.

52. McCabe's letter is quoted in Hubbell, pp. 14-15. Letter to Rachel Lyons, August 12, 1863, *Alabama Review*, II, p. 148. Timrod many times complained of suffering from the heat; in the August letter, for example, he wrote that "July, August, and September are

left out of my poetical year." This inability to write distressed him greatly; on June 21, 1863, he had complained to Rachel that, although occasionally "stirred by the breeze of poesy," otherwise "my spirit has become a Dead Sea into which no Jordan flows."

53. Letter to Hayne, July 20, 1864; quoted in Hubbell, pp. 36-37. The Columbia *Daily South Carolinian* on January 13, 1864, announced the transfer of ownership from R. W. Gibbes to F. G. De Fontaine and Co., and that "For an associate editor we have secured the services of HENRY TIMROD, ESQ. With a name linked to the memory of some of the sweetest poems of our land, and with a pen fruitful in the beautiful imagery of the sentiments and affections, there will be at least one department of the *Carolinian* which will have its constant and gratified readers." A few days before February 10, 1862 (letter to Emily), Timrod had "had the pleasure to sup" with De Fontaine, and he described him as "a handsome young fellow of West Indian parentage—clever but superficial and evidently a mere Bohemian."

54. Letter to W. A. Courtenay, March 7, 1901, bound in *Memories of the Timrod Revival*. "A Theory of Poetry" is reprinted from Timrod's manuscript (Charleston Library Society) in *The Essays of Henry Timrod,* pp. 103-32; for bibliographical details, see *Essays,* pp. 165-66.

55. There were two announcements in the *Carolinian,* one factual and one humorous. The first: "In Columbia, on the 16th instant, by the Reverend J. Maxwell Pringle, Henry Timrod, of Charleston, S. C., to Miss Katie S. Goodwin, youngest daughter of the late George Marriott Goodwin, Esquire, of Bury St. Edmunds, England." The second, almost certainly by the sardonic De Fontaine: "Another Defunct Bachelor.—It is with a species of grim satisfaction that we announce in our columns today another diminution in the ranks of single blesseddom. . . . Henry Timrod by name—poet, dreamer, philosopher, and good fellow generally, after suffering for months all the horrors of that worst of 'ills that flesh is heir to'—enlargement of the heart—has at last entered his haven of rest." Timrod had been a "nervous, restless, jerky, abstracted individual who was wont to upset our exchanges, read papers for hours upside down, write editorials and tear them up." Timrod and his bride had departed temporarily "into the profundities of Georgia"—one of the very few references to a honeymoon of any kind.

56. Simms, *Letters,* IV, pp. 450-51.

57. Letter from Hayne to Clara Dargan, April 23, 1870; quoted in Hubbell, p. 17. In the *Memoir,* p. 43, Hayne suppressed this feeling entirely: "It is pleasant to dwell upon his honeymoon and the few months immediately succeeding it." Timrod's letters to Hayne are

quoted in Hubbell, pp. 30-33 and 36-39; the second letter to Clara Dargan, August 20, 1864, also in Hubbell, pp. 40-41.

58. Letters to Hayne, July 10, 1864, and August 25, 1864; in Hubbell, pp. 30-34 and 41-43. As early as June 18, 1860, he had written to Emily (letter in South Caroliniana Library): "Keep me advised of Mr. G's health—you have made me uneasy." For Simms' distrust of Davidson, see Simms, *Letters*, IV, pp. 460-61.

59. Hayne, p. 44. In his ornate style, Hayne adds: "A few weeks of dalliance with his infant beauty; of undisturbed calm in the little nest of a home he had reared for himself and his wife, and then came fearful reports of invasion; the rapid, overwhelming march of the enemy, and upon the 17th of February, 1865 (just one year *and a day* since Timrod's marriage) the devoted city of Columbia was given up to the mercies of Sherman and his troops."

60. Julian A. Selby, *Memorabilia and Anecdotal Reminiscences of Columbia, S. C., and Incidents Connected Therewith* (Columbia, 1905), p. 101; Hayne, p. 45. I have been unable to find documentary evidence, but this seems to have been the time when Timrod took refuge at "Forest Cottage," four miles from Florence, S. C. (Thompson, p. 22).

61. Timrod wrote (March 30, 1866; Hubbell, p. 60) to Hayne that since Sherman's raid, "I have been residing with my sister." J. P. Thomas quotes this, in his "Timrod's Checkered Career," Charleston *Sunday News*, March 5 and 12, 1899; the articles are by a man who had known Timrod, but mainly follows Hayne and Bruns. Timrod wrote to R. H. Stoddard, on July 10 and Sept. 8, 1865; these have been published in Douglas J. Robillard's "Two Timrod Letters," *North Carolina Historical Review*, XXXIX (Autumn, 1962), pp. 549-53. In the first, Timrod noted that "It is about six years ago since you favored me with a very kind letter upon the appearance of a small volume of poems of mine, a copy of which volume I had caused to be sent to you." Illness had prevented Timrod's answering the 1860 letter. Stoddard answered the July letter cordially; at his request Timrod sent in September his poems of a non-war nature—all he had on hand "likely to be acceptable." Of these, only "An Exotic" (a tribute to Katie, written and published before they were married) is named. Timrod was dilatory about mailing the letter; on Oct. 1st, he added a postscript that the illness of his wife and sister had caused him to neglect mailing it. Stoddard consolidated the information in the two letters, treating them as though they were one letter, in his article-review of the Hayne edition of Timrod's poems in *The Aldine*, April, 1873; this version is quoted in Hubbell, pp. 46-48. One error crept into the magazine text. Timrod had written that "Literature is an unattainable and undesired luxury," not an "undesirable luxury."

Hubbell also quotes from a Hayne letter to Stoddard (February 14, 1860): "I cannot tell you how sincerely gratified I am, to find, that my friend's vol. has not merely satisfied but 'charmed' you. Timrod possesses more ability, (native, and acquired,)—than all the other young poets of the South, placed together. For myself, (loving the man as I would a brother)—, his successes are my successes,—all his triumphs—mine." Hayne almost repeats this in a letter to Whittier, March 23, 1870: "You have characterized his later poems with discriminating taste." Hayne speaks of Timrod as "my friend, my more than brother". (Duke University Library).

62. Letter to Hayne, March 30, 1866. Emily's husband, George Goodwin, and Henry's youngest sister, Edyth Cotchett, died in 1865. I have tried to indicate later that I think "A Mother's Wail" is artistically objectified, for all its personal tone; Walter Hines Page (*South Atlantic*, I, p. 367) wrote of it that "I am not sure but that it is the nearest perfect of all. . . . To the reader of Simonides it seems almost Greek-like."

63. Letter to Hayne, March 30, 1866; quoted in Hubbell, pp. 59-63. It is not certain who bought the few remaining books. Thompson, pp. 42-43, writes that Simms bought them; Charles H. Ross in "The New Edition of Timrod," *Sewanee Review*, VII (October, 1899), pp. 414-20, thought that Alfred W. Austin bought them and sent them to Simms to be sold for Timrod's benefit. Letters from Arthur Williams Austin (in the Ferris Collection, Columbia University Library, and one privately owned by C. Waller Barrett) describe various gifts that he sent to the Simms family. Austin, who lived at "Cedar Hill," near Boston, is the most likely purchaser. Ross justly criticizes the arrangement of Timrod's poems and the inadequate Introduction, but his review is disappointingly thin. Several of Timrod's best poems were published in Simms' *War Poetry of the South* (1867).

64. Letter to Edith Goodwin, from Columbia, April 16, 1866; in South Caroliniana Library. Edith was tutoring or teaching near Orangeburg, possibly at Murray Robinson's plantation, for Timrod asks her to remember him to Mr. and Mrs. Robinson and the boys; he hoped that she and her pupils had enjoyed their holiday in Charleston.

65. I have used the advertisement that appeared on September 23, 1866. In a letter to Hayne, November 23, 1867, Emily noted that during this period Timrod worked briefly as assistant clerk in a United States Court—she thought it was the Court of Common Pleas. That it was a temporary position is indicated by the fact that no record of his employment seems to be in existence.

66. Letter from Simms to Hayne, October 22, 1866; in Simms,

Letters, IV, p. 614. He prefaces this with: "Poor Timrod is the very prince of Dolefuls, and swallowed up in distresses. . . . He can earn nothing where he is—goes to bed hungry every night—, and suffers from bad health. It is the mortifying thing to all of us, that *none* of *us* can help him. Bruns and myself are both living from hand to mouth, and not infrequently the hand carries nothing to the cavernous receptacle." On November 29 (IV, p. 622) he noted: "Timrod has been on the verge of starvation. He is now acting as private secty. to Governor Orr," and on April 3, 1867 (V, p. 40) that Timrod was "still, at intervals" the Governor's private secretary, "who pays him $100 a month, while he employs him." Timrod's picture of his work is less glamorous. On November 19, 1866, he wrote to Hayne (*Memoir,* pp. 51-52) that "Your letter found me a scribe in the Governor's Office, where I work every day from 9 A.M. to 7 P.M. . . . just as I was about to despair of help from God or man, I received from Governor Orr a temporary appointment as an assistant secretary, or, rather, clerk. The appointment is but for a month or so, in order to get through a certain amount of work that crowds upon the department at this time." To Judge Bryan, Timrod wrote in January, 1867: "My term of service in the Executive office ended with the close of the session. It was no child's play. On *two* occasions I wrote *from 10 o'clock one morning* until the sunrise of the next day."

67. Letters to Hayne, March 7, 1867, and March 26, 1867; quoted in Hubbell, pp. 55 and 75. Emily's letter to Hayne was written November 21, 1867, after Henry's death. The letters to Thompson are in the A. W. Anthony Collection, New York Public Library, and are printed in Douglas J. Robillard, "Henry Timrod, John R. Thompson, and the Ladies of Richmond," *South Carolina Historical Magazine,* LXII (1961), pp. 129-33. Hayne, p. 54, quotes from an April, 1867, letter of Timrod's, now apparently lost: "*Apropos* of literature and rhymesters, I have lately had a *modest* request by a committee of Richmond ladies, intent upon establishing a Bazaar, or something, in that city. It was, to write within a fortnight, a poem on the history of 'Fort Sumter,' beginning with the shot at the 'Star of the West,' and ending with the elevation of the United States flag over the ruins of the fort! This poem I was further requested to make long enough to fill *eighty printed octavo pages,* or—it was obligingly qualified—less!! Need I say that I respectfully declined the task."

68. Hayne, pp. 53-55; Hubbell, p. 83.

69. Hubbell, pp. 85, 88. This may have been Julian A. Selby, but more probably was Charles P. Pelham, who had published the *Southern Guardian* in Columbia before the war; as early as March 30, 1866, Timrod wrote Hayne that "Pelham is about to issue the

Guardian once more, and I have some hope that he will offer me its editorial chair."

70. Letter to Hayne, July 4 and July 11, 1867; quoted in Hubbell, pp. 82-84, 89. Mrs. Goodwin, in a letter to Hayne written on November 25, 1867, was equally indignant with Simms:

He never did and never could appreciate or understand the shrinking refined and sensitive nature of my brother. While the latter was on a visit to you last summer Mr. Simms called to see us on his way North. Notwithstanding I assured him that Hal was really ill, too ill to work, too ill almost to think, Mr. Simms said, "He is lazy, Timrod was always lazy. When in Charleston instead of writing he would lie in bed reading yellow papered novels." I shall never forget Hal's indignation when I told him this. You know how much of his time could have been passed in reading novels who had attained so great a height in scholarship.

71. M. B. Siegler, *op. cit.*, pp. 178-79. Sophie's mother had offered a teaching job in Athens, Georgia, to Emily; but on September 10, 1866, she felt forced to decline, as Henry could not get a job, and if she accepted "I should have to turn him and Katie into the street."

72. Letter to Clara Dargan, August 7, 1867; quoted in Hubbell, p. 90.

73. Hayne, pp. 56-57. On this second trip, Timrod hoped (letter from "Copse Hill," August 20, 1867) to visit his niece Edith in Athens, but was too physically weak to do so. The chief attraction "yourself—though I like the old town for the sake of many a pleasant memory."

Trent, who had access to letters that have since been lost, wrote (p. 306) that the letters Simms received from Timrod "during the months preceding the latter's decease are too harrowing to bear quotation. The evils inflicted by poverty were bad enough, but the consciousness that he was dying by inches, and the suffering occasioned by a severe and, perhaps, carelessly performed, operation had rendered the last year of the young poet's life simply unendurable."

In response to a charge by Dr. F. Muensch of Charleston that Timrod died of starvation, Julian A. Selby denied this: Timrod "died of consumption, which was connected with some other disease," and this second disease brought on attacks of such fury that Timrod "was scarcely manageable" (Columbia *State*, January 16, 1898). Emily, on September 29, 1867, wrote to Hayne that "Dr. Gibbes told me this morning, that he had no doubt Hal's was a case of confirmed bronchitis" (South Caroliniana Library).

74. Letter to Hayne, September 13 and September 16, 1867; quoted in Hubbell, pp. 91-93; Hayne, pp. 58-60; Thompson, pp.

48-49. The sonnet was published in the Charleston *Courier*, October 4, 1867, and in the Columbia *Daily Phoenix*, October 8, 1867. Emily hoped (to Hayne, October 15, 1867) that "an inheritor to the name and genius of our Southern poet may yet be given us." The hope proved vain. Henry Rives Polland was the editor of *Southern Opinion*. The bloodstained proofsheets are in the Charleston Library Society.

75. Hayne, pp. 61-65; Hubbell, pp. 94-97. Edyth Timrod Cotchett had been buried in the same plot in 1865. Emily wrote to Hayne (May 18, 1870) that Mrs. William Henry Timrod, their mother, died in Columbia on April 15, 1870; she is buried alongside Henry and Willie. Emily died in 1872 in Washington, where she was staying with her sister-in-law Katie. Before her mother died, Emily had made a living by boarding several federal officers, with the result that she was "subsequently isolated in Columbia." Katie secured a job in the Treasury Department at a salary of $900 a year. Emily was suffering from asthma and general debility; on September 25, 1872, she wrote Hayne from Washington that this probably was the "last letter I shall ever write you; I grow daily so much worse." Katie Timrod was married again, to a Mr. Lloyd; she died at Ridgefield Park, New Jersey, on March 20, 1913.

Chapter Two

1. All of this material is in the bound volume, *Autographic Relics*, in the Courtenay Collection, Charleston Library Society. For documentation, I have hereafter listed this book as Cardwell, followed by the page number. When a reference to Timrod's early volume has seemed needed, I have shortened it to *1859 Poems;* for the Hayne edition, to Hayne; and for the Memorial Edition—which I have used when possible, since it is the most readily available—to *Poems. The Essays of Henry Timrod* I have also shortened to *Essays*. Whenever feasible, I have from this point placed documentation in the text.

2. Hayne, p. 19; Cardwell, *Uncollected Poems*, pp. 40, 53-54. Cardwell has listed the sonnet beginning "How Many Yearn to Tear Aside the Veil" as appearing over the initials T. H. in the Charleston *Evening News*, September 8, 1846; to this should be added the poem "Eyes," same signature, Charleston *Evening News*, September 16, 1846. In *Autographic Relics* and in Cardwell the title is "Choice of Eyes." H. T. Thompson, p. 89, wrote that "Florabel" had appeared "originally" in the Charleston *Evening News* and "was written when Timrod was a college boy." However, he gives no record and cites no authority. Cardwell, p. 112, lists its first publication as in the *Charleston College Magazine*, II (April, 1855), pp. 18-19.

3. Hayne, p. 19; John Dickson Bruns, "A Lecture on Timrod,"

Charleston *Sunday News* (printed in full, April 30, 1899; delivered October 27, 1870); Ludwig Lewisohn, *Books We Have Made*, Chap. XII, Charleston *News and Courier*, July 5–September 20, 1903; J. B. Hubbell, *The South in American Literature*, pp. 468-69. The pair of sonnets to Arabella (Mrs. Theodore C. Caskin of New York) apparently were popular; at least, they were widely reprinted. Her birthday fell on the same day of the month as Henry's. See Cardwell, p. 116, n. 27.

    4. Hayne, pp. 20-21; Cardwell, pp. 51, 53.
    5. Hubbell, *Timrod*, pp. 70-71, where Hayne's letter is quoted; Cardwell, pp. 7n., 119. Thompson in turn admired Timrod's poetry: "When I read his poems, I feel so deep a sense of utter inferiority that I almost vow I will never write another line," letter to Hayne, March 22, 1867; quoted in Hubbell, p. 73. One other poem signed "Aglaus" should be added to Cardwell's checklist of magazine publication: "Song—We walk'd beneath the shadow," in *Southern Literary Gazette*, Athens, Ga., II (Sept. 1, 1849), p. 18; it is in *Autographic Relics* and is reprinted in Cardwell, pp. 44-45.
    6. *Poems*, pp. 100-1; Hayne, pp. 20-21 and 162. The friend was Hayne. H. T. Thompson, p. 117, identifies the Northern writer as John Greenleaf Whittier. For several letters that express Whittier's admiration for Timrod's poetry, see Hubbell, pp. 111-20; the most significant one in this connection was a reply to a charge of prejudice, made after Hayne's death: "I was one of the very first to recognize the rare gifts of the Carolinian poet Timrod, and I was an intimate friend of the lamented Paul H. Hayne, though both wrote lyrics against the North" (Samuel T. Pickard, *Life and Letters of John Greenleaf Whittier*, 1894, II, p. 502). Henry Austin, in *The Bookman*, IX (June, 1899), p. 343, thought that some of Timrod's lines reminded one of Whittier. Emily wrote to Hayne, May 18, 1870, that "the last verses Hal ever read to me were lines by Whittier" from "Snow-Bound." See Hubbell, pp. 111-17.
    7. Hayne, pp. 30-31. "A Vision of Poesy," which first appeared in the *1859 Poems*, is reprinted in the Memorial Edition, pp. 74-100. For quotations from Shelley's "Alastor," I have used *The Poetical Works of Percy Bysshe Shelley* (edited by Mrs. Shelley, Boston, 1881), I, pp. 157-66. Several critics have thought they detected a stronger indebtedness to Shelley than I can find. Peirce Bruns, in the *Conservative Review*, I (May, 1899), pp. 263-77, makes the strongest statement that I have seen; he thinks there is little resemblance between Wordsworth's handling of nature and Timrod's: "Timrod, in this regard, at least, is far nearer to Shelley." I do not agree with this statement.
    8. Timrod expressed something of the same idea in "Youth and

Manhood," which first appeared in the *Southern Literary Gazette*, November 27, 1852; in *Poems*, pp. 24-26. Here he emphasizes the disillusionment of manhood, the realization that however high pinnacles may rise, "None touch the sky." If the young poet cannot keep his faith, then he asks God to "Give me to chant one pure and deathless lay,/And let me die."

9. Hayne, pp. 23-24; *Essays*, p. 39.

10. *Poems*, pp. 103-4; Thompson, p. 111. For other examples of direct indebtedness to Tennyson, see especially "Hark to the Shouting Wind" (*Poems*, pp. 26-27) and "Lines to R. L.", (*Poems*, pp. 131-32). In a letter to Rachel Lyons, June 9, 1861 (already quoted), Timrod indicated that the theme of an Arctic voyage continued to fascinate him, but that he feared to undertake the work until his poetic powers "shall have attained their utmost strength."

11. *Poems*, pp. 20-23. The person supposed to be speaking addresses Timrod interchangeably as Harry or Hal; these were the names most frequently used by Timrod's friends. The proofsheets, stanza 4, line 2, have "Two blue eyes" instead of "Two dark eyes." Whether Hayne or Timrod made the change is unknown.

12. *Poems*, pp. 28-30. A closely related work, probably written also in 1858, is "A Trifle" (*Poems*, p. 190). It was not published until after Timrod's death, in *Appletons' Journal*, March 22, 1873.

13. *Poems*, pp. 46-57; first published in *Harper's*, August, 1860. Hayne divided the poem into three parts; in the proofsheets there are only two parts. Timrod also wrote for her the poem "Sophie," in Cardwell, pp. 97-98.

14. "A Rhapsody of a Southern Winter Night," in *Poems*, pp. 109-13; published in *Russell's*, July, 1857. The letter is to Rachel Lyons, July 23, 1863; in S L M, II (December, 1940), p. 651.

15. I have drawn some of this material from my longer article, "Timrod's Concept·of Dreams," *South Atlantic Quarterly*, XLVIII (October, 1949), pp. 584-88.

16. W. G. Simms, "The Late Henry Timrod," *Southern Society*, I (Oct. 12, 1867), pp. 18-19; in Hubbell, pp. 152-65; quotation on p. 157. J. D. Bruns, "A Lecture on Timrod," Charleston *Sunday News*, April 30, 1899. Hayne, p. 29; Hubbell, p. 9.

17. Bruns, *op. cit.* W. J. Rivers, pp. 10-11, noted that Timrod could not write verses "unless he had personally known the occasion, unless his own soul had felt and the instinctive spirit of song had been stirred within him. This truthfulness to his own heart, this reverence for nature as she was revealed to him, secured to his effusions an absence from affectation and from the imitation of the writings of others. This is the source of his excellence."

Chapter Three

1. "A Vision of Poesy" has been discussed in Chap. II. See also his sonnet, "Poet! if on a lasting fame be bent," *Poems*, p. 169, published in *S L M*, July, 1849.

2. See especially "Vox et Praeterea Nihil," "Retirement," and the sonnet beginning, "They dub thee idler," in *Poems*, pp. 31-32, 136-37, and 172; and the sonnet, "In the Deep Shadow," Cardwell, p. 53. I have discussed this feeling in the Introduction, *Essays*, pp. 24-26.

3. In *Russell's*, I (May, 1857), pp. 156-59; reprinted in *Essays*, pp. 61-68. The quotation from Hayne is from his *Memoir*, p. 26.

4. Grayson's article was published in *Russell's*, I (July, 1857), pp. 327-37; reprinted in Timrod's *Essays*, pp. 135-54. With a few changes and additions, it forms Chap. XI of Grayson's autobiography, in the South Caroliniana Library and published in the *South Carolina Historical and Genealogical Magazine*, July, 1947-April, 1950. In the Preface to his book-length poem, *The Hireling and The Slave* (1854), Grayson noted that he had attempted to give "some variety to the poetic forms that are almost universally prevalent" by returning to the "School of Dryden and Pope."

5. Timrod's "What Is Poetry?" appeared in *Russell's*, II (October, 1857), pp. 52-58; reprinted in *Essays*, pp. 69-82. Joseph Le Conte's article, "On the Nature and Uses of Art," appeared in the *Southern Presbyterian Review*, XV (Jan., 1863), pp. 519-20.

6. "Literature in the South" was published in *Russell's*, V (August, 1859), pp. 385-95; reprinted in *Essays*, pp. 83-102. Timrod had used it as a lecture at Cheraw, S. C., and possibly elsewhere. The best study of the efforts to foster Southern literature is Jay B. Hubbell's "Literary Nationalism in the Old South," in *American Studies in Honor of William Kenneth Boyd* (Durham, 1940), pp. 175-220; quotation on p. 208.

7. Letter from Timrod to Emily Goodwin, July 29, 1863, in South Caroliniana Library.

8. Letter to Rachel Lyons, July 7, 1861, in *S L M*, II (November, 1940), pp. 605-6. On April 13, 1867, he wrote to Hayne that "I have read (skippingly) St. Elmo. Somebody lent it to my wife." Timrod thought poorly of the book and its author: "I met her, you know, in Mobile—took tea with her several evenings in succession. She talks well, but pedantically now and then; though not so pedantically as she writes. She has very peculiar, but very false and shallow opinions about poetry and poets."

9. Letter to Emily, March 25, 1861, South Caroliniana Library.

Apparently Edyth was not persuaded. W. A. Courtenay wrote that she "was gifted with a mind very much like that of her brother and composed beautiful verse. She had collected them in a book in manuscript form, but it was lost. They were too poor to keep their treasures safely" (newspaper clipping, "The Grave of Henry Timrod is Suitably Marked," in Courtenay Collection, Charleston Library Society).

10. Given as a lecture at Columbia, S. C., during the winter of 1863-64; reprinted from Timrod's manuscript in the Charleston Library Society in *Essays*, pp. 103-32.

11. Columbia *Daily South Carolinian*, January 19, 1864.

12. Letter to Hayne, July 10, 1864; quoted in Hubbell, p. 32: "I do not know whether you have published any verses lately, but if so, you may possibly be surprised that they are not copied in the Carolinian. The reason is that I never see a literary paper. Fontaine immediately seizes on them for his wife who keeps them on file."

13. "Southern Nationality," January 16, 1864; reprinted in Hubbell, pp. 135-37.

14. "Southern Literature," January 14, 1864; reprinted in Hubbell, pp. 133-35, and in *Essays*, pp. 162-63.

15. "Nationality in Literature," January 19, 1864; reprinted in Hubbell, pp. 137-40, and in *Essays*, pp. 160-61.

16. "National Songs," January 24, 1864; reprinted in Hubbell, pp. 140-42, and in *Essays*, pp. 163-64. See also his letter to Rachel Lyons, September 6, 1861, in *S L M*, II (November, 1940), p. 609.

17. "War and Literature," February 28, 1864; reprinted in Hubbell, pp. 142-45, and in *Essays*, pp. 168-69. See also an untitled editorial of September 15, 1864, reprinted in *Essays*, pp. 169-70.

18. Editorial, *Daily South Carolinian*, August 3, 1864. His most extensive use of Shakespearean characters is in "Address Delivered at the Opening of the New Theatre at Richmond," in *Poems*, pp. 69-73. It was first published in *S L M*, February, 1863.

19. "The Grandeur of the Struggle," February 27, 1864; reprinted in Hubbell, pp. 145-47.

20. "South Carolinian Refugees," April 19, 1864; reprinted in Hubbell, pp. 147-51.

21. Hayne, pp. 47-51. Thompson reprints the same editorials, and a section from "The Sonnet," pp. 129-37. "The Alabama" appeared in the *Daily South Carolinian*, March 8, 1864.

22. Letter to Hayne, August 25, 1864; printed in Hubbell, pp. 41-43. "The Troubles of a Mid Summer Night" appeared in the City Items column, August 14 and 16, 1864; "Arsenal Hill," August 13, 1864. A paragraph by Timrod, "Spring," had appeared in City Items, April 28, 1864.

23. Letter to Hayne, March 7, 1867; in Hubbell, pp. 51-56 (who warned me that the letter was mistakenly dated 1866). Timrod declared here that he liked "to plunge *in medias res*"; in an earlier letter (March 30, 1866), he remarked that "I have the right poet's inclination to plunge at once *in medias res.*"

24. Letter to Hayne, July 11, 1867; quoted in Hubbell, pp. 87-88. Hayne's prize poem was "The Confederates in the Field"; Timrod's, "Address Delivered at the Opening of the New Theatre at Richmond."

Chapter Four

1. Rivers, *A Little Book*, p. 17; Letter, Timrod to Stoddard, July 10, 1865; quoted by Stoddard in a review of the Hayne edition of Timrod's *Poems, Aldine*, April, 1873; reprinted in Hubbell, pp. 46-48; Letter, Hayne to Rossiter Johnson, October 10, 1876; printed in Hubbell, pp. 105-10.

2. *Poems, pp.* 150-54. As "Ode on Occasion of the meeting of the Southern Congress," it appeared in *Littell's Living Age*, March 30, 1861; as "Ode, on the Meeting of the Southern Congress" as a broadside (copy in the Harris Collection, John Hay Library, Brown University); in the Charleston *Mercury*, September 26, 1861; and in Charleston *Courier*, January 31, 1862—the *Courier* version, he complained to Rachel Lyons in a letter of February 3, 1862, S L M, II (December, 1940), p. 645, "under the sesquipedalian title of *Ethnogenesis . . .* with emendations." For the public reading, see Thompson, p. 32.

3. *Poems*, pp. 6-11; first published in the Charleston *Mercury*, March 4, 1862. In a letter of August 20, 1861, S L M, II (November, 1940), p. 608, he wrote to Rachel Lyons that she might "look soon for a poem entitled 'The Cotton-Boll'—but where, I cannot tell you—certainly however in the paper which I think will pay me the highest price." That he soon lost faith in cotton is indicated in a letter to Emily Goodwin, February 25, 1862; the passage is significant enough to bear requoting: "I begin to despair of European intervention. We have over-rated the power of King Cotton. When King Wheat gets upon his throne, he is just as strong."

4. Letter to Rachel Lyons, August 20, 1861, S L M, II (November, 1940), pp. 607-8. It was printed in the Charleston *Mercury*, October 7, 1861, and in the *Courier*, December 19, 1861. Timrod revised the sonnet extensively for the proofsheets; this later version is given in Hayne, pp. 202-3, and in *Poems*, p. 177. The major changes are in the second through the fifth lines; in the 1861 version,

> I know not why, but all this weary day,
> Sad fancies have been flitting through my brain;

My very books suggested shapes of pain.
Sometimes it was a vessel losing way
Rounding a stormy cape; sometimes a gray
Dull waste of clouds above a wintry main;

Timrod's revisions strengthened the early impression:

I know not why, but all this weary day,
Suggested by no definite grief or pain,
Sad fancies have been flitting through my brain;
Now it has been a vessel losing way,
Rounding a stormy headland; now a gray
Dull waste of clouds above a wintry main;

Timrod's attitude toward the war as a source of inspiration varied; he wrote his niece Edith as late as April 28, 1863 (South Caroliniana Library) that he had hoped to write some verses for her; but his Muse had proved a jade that had obstinately "refused for some time to open her lips except to chant rebellious sentiments, and martial laments and triumphs."

5. Letter to Emily Goodwin, June 11, 1861; letter to Rachel Lyons, December 25, 1861, *S L M*, II (November, 1940), pp. 609-11. He hoped his poetic extravagances would not harm Katie in Rachel's estimation.

6. *Poems,* pp. 38-44; first published in Charleston *Mercury,* December 28, 1861, and the *Courier,* December 28, 1861; and as a separate illustrated book by E. J. Hale and Son, Boston, 1884. On February 3, 1862, Timrod sent Rachel an "emended edition of 'Katie.'" He also wrote, but apparently never published, an eight-line poem, "My Katie"; the only copy I have seen is written in Timrod's hand on white satin, and is in the Charleston Library Society; printed in Cardwell, p. 102.

7. Letter to Rachel Lyons, December 25, 1861, *S L M*, II (November, 1940), pp. 610-11. In the last section of "Katie" Timrod wrote, describing Katie's birthplace:

Has not the sky a deeper blue,
Have not the trees a greener hue,

Byron, in the first stanza of "Parasina," described the lovers at evening:

And in the sky the stars are met,
And on the wave is deeper blue,
And on the leaf a browner hue.

8. Letter to Rachel Lyons, February 3, 1862, *S L M*, II (December, 1940), p. 645. Timrod had sent it earlier, on January 20, 1862,

for he notes: "I am glad to hear that you like 'Rachel,'" and added that the poem had appeared in the *Courier* "a fortnight ago" (January 23, 1862; also in the *Mercury*, January 29, 1862). All the published versions have had the title "La Belle Juive." If "Lines to R. L." are the same or a revised version of the lines in her diary, they first appeared in Hayne, New Revised Version, pp. 221-22; in *Poems*, pp. 131-32. In this letter Timrod notes: "I have been amused by a mistake which a Virginia paper makes in the first verse. It reads in very bad type:

> 'Is it because your sable hair
> Is folded over brows that wear
> At times a too *important* air? ! ! '

How do you like the variation? I laughed heartily at it myself—though at the same time I was not a little annoyed at the absurdity of the blunder." The correct reading is "a too imperial air." There is no record as to whether or not Rachel was amused.

9. *Poems*, pp. 59-61. In a letter to Emily Timrod Goodwin, April 11, 1862, Timrod wrote that it was because of Katie that he was going as war correspondent to the western theatre: "But for my engagement to Katie, I would have preferred to remain idle in Keitt's camp. But I owe it to the dear girl to show that I have energy and a capacity—when I choose to exert it to go through the world as boldly and determinedly as the most leather-headed, thick-skinned of those who pride themselves on their 'savoir faire.' Katie is my inspiration and my strength." The poem, "An Exotic," was published in the Charleston *Mercury*, July 12, 1862.

10. Letter to Rachel Lyons, February 6, 1862, S L M, II (December, 1940), pp. 646-47. "A Cry to Arms" did not appear in the Charleston *Mercury* and the Charleston *Courier* until March 4, 1862, so this was evidently a manuscript version; in *Poems*, pp. 144-46. "Carolina" appeared in the *Courier*, March 8, 1862; in *Poems*, pp. 141-44.

11. Hayne, pp. 37-38; Wauchope, p. 28.

12. Letters to Rachel Lyons, February 21, April 8, and April 15, 1862, S L M, II (December, 1940), pp. 647-50; letter to Emily, April 11, 1862 (South Caroliniana Library); letter of Mrs. Rachel Lyons Heustis to W. A. Courtenay, written in 1899 and in the Courtenay Collection, Charleston Library Society. See also J. D. Bruns, "A Lecture on Timrod"; Bruns pictured Timrod as a child "suddenly flung into the heart of that stormy retreat, and tossed like a straw on the crest of those waves from which he escaped as by a miracle."

13. Letters to Rachel Lyons, July 25, and October 28, 1862, *Ala-*

bama Review, II (April, 1949), pp. 139-49; Thompson, p. 35.

14. "Serenade" appeared in the Charleston *Courier,* November 12, 1862; in the *Mercury,* December 19, 1863; in the *Daily South Carolinian,* May 18, 1864; in *Poems,* p. 23. Letter to Rachel Lyons, November, 1862. In the first stanza, the lover addresses the curtain at his sweetheart's window.

15. First published in the Charleston *Mercury,* December 13, 1862: in *Poems,* pp. 146-48. Louis D. Rubin's article, "Henry Timrod and the Dying of the Light," was published in the *Mississippi Quarterly,* XI (Summer, 1958), pp. 101-11; it deserves reading, and may seem more convincing to other readers than to me. As early as February 25, 1862, Timrod was assuring Emily that Charleston was "in no immediate danger," since the Northern fleet was "destined for the ports of the Gulf." But he was distressed that city and military authorities had done so little in getting fortifications ready: "the city is only safe through the sufferance of the enemy." He regretted that it was "impossible to persuade Ma and Rebecca to leave the city at present."

16. *Poems,* pp. 148-50; first published in the Charleston *Mercury,* December 11, 1862. Brig.-Gen. Roswell Sabine Ripley (1823-87) had graduated from the U. S. Military Academy in 1843 and had first "won his fame" at Vera Cruz in the Mexican War. Although a native of Ohio, he joined the Confederate Army; and, when the poem was written, he was in command of all the Confederate forces in South Carolina.

17. *Poems,* pp. 160-63; first published in the Charleston *Mercury,* December 25, 1862. F. G. De Fontaine, in the Charleston *Sunday News,* June 28, 1896, records an interview with W. A. Courtenay, who remembered that Longfellow, after reading aloud "the beautiful invocation to Peace," closed the book of Timrod's poems with the remark, "I do not wonder . . . that Tennyson exclaimed, 'The man who wrote those lines deserves to be called the poet laureate of the south!'" Ellison Capers, Episcopal Bishop of South Carolina, thought it Timrod's finest poem; and he included it in an article in *The Churchman,* November 18, 1877. Both in "Charleston" and in "Christmas," Timrod is indebted to Tennyson's "In Memoriam," esp. section XI.

18. Emily Goodwin wrote to Hayne, November 23, 1867 (when a collected edition of Timrod's poems was first being planned) that Henry had intended this to be the first poem in the projected English book, and that she wished it to be put first in the Hayne edition. Hayne readily acceded. For some reason, in the chaotically arranged Memorial Edition, it appears as #14, pp. 36-38 (immediately before

"Katie"). Since three poems, including one to Sophie Sosnowski and one to Rachel Lyons, separate "Katie" and "An Exotic," a grouping by unity of person seems improbable.

19. *Poems*, pp. 3-5; *Southern Illustrated News*, April 4, 1863. The quotation from J. P. K. Bryan is on p. xxxvi; if Bryan arranged the order of the poems, his preference for "Spring" may have been indicated by his placing it first in the Memorial Edition, instead of among the war poems.

20. "Carmen Triumphale," *Poems*, pp. 154-56; *Southern Illustrated News*, June 7, 1863.

21. Letters to Rachel Lyons, July 23, 1863, August 12, 1863, and September 30, 1863; *S L M*, II (December, 1940), pp. 650-51, and *Alabama Review*, II (April, 1949), pp. 139-49; Hubbell, pp. 14-15, quotes from William Gordon McCabe's *Journal*, August 23, 1863: "I became acquainted tonight with Henry Timrod, the southern poet. He is a small, melancholy-looking man, black moustache, grey eyes, and sallow complexion. Very pleasant he is in conversation." McCabe makes it plain that Timrod was with a newspaper, but he does not mention its name.

22. Emily wrote to Hayne that he moved to Columbia on January 12, 1864. The *Daily South Carolinian*, January 13, 1864, announced that Timrod would be associate editor (previously quoted). For the anonymous sonnet, see Cardwell, p. 102. But see also Timrod's letter to Hayne, August 25, 1864 (in Hubbell, pp. 41-43); for the anonymous sonnet, Hubbell, pp. 125, 131; Cardwell, p. 7. I think this sonnet was by Timrod, but I disagree with Hubbell and Cardwell in that I think he was infuriated by criticism of his wife rather than of himself. The sonnet "We may not falter" appeared first in the *Daily South Carolinian*, January 15, 1864; it is reprinted in Cardwell, pp. 102-3. His fear that he could no longer write poetry was expressed in a letter to Hayne, August 25, 1864; the "Hymn," which was published in the *Daily South Carolinian*, November 6, 1864, is also in *Poems*, p. 130.

23. *Poems*, pp. 164-65. Perhaps the full subtitle should be given: "Sung on the Occasion of Decorating the Graves of the Confederate Dead, at Magnolia Cemetery, Charleston, S. C., 1867." G. P. Voigt, in "New Light on Timrod's 'Memorial Ode'," *American Literature*, IV (January, 1933), pp. 395-96, first pointed out (at least in modern times) that the ode was actually sung on June 16, 1866. It was printed in the Charleston *Courier* two days later, and the revised version on July 23. Hayne and, of course, the Memorial Edition after him follow the first version, although with changes in punctuation; Hayne may well have followed a text furnished him by Emily or by

Katie. I should note that Dr. Jay B. Hubbell, in *The South in American Literature,* p. 474, and in *American Life in Literature,* vol. I, has also reprinted the revised text.

24. This obituary appeared in *Scott's Monthly Magazine,* Atlanta, IV (October, 1867), pp. 832-33. "The Rosebuds" was published in *Scott's,* II (July, 1866), p. 520; Hayne, pp. 111-12; and in *Poems,* pp. 61-62. "Two Rosebuds" is sometimes given as the title.

25. "Our Willie" appeared in *Scott's,* II (September, 1866), pp. 706-7; in *Poems,* pp. 64-68; "A Mother's Wail," *Scott's,* II (October, 1866), p. 742; in *Poems,* pp. 62-64. The John R. Thompson letter to Hayne, March 22, 1867, is quoted in Hubbell, pp. 72-74. Walter Hines Pages, in the *South-Atlantic,* I (March, 1867), p. 367, thought it Timrod's most nearly perfect poem.

26. The sonnet, beginning "Life ever seems," is in *Poems,* p. 171; in *Scott's,* II (November, 1866), p. 855. It was republished in *Southern Opinion,* February 22, 1868. For the letter to Hayne, September 13, 1867, see Hubbell, p. 91-92; for the text of the poem described below, pp. 131-32. The little poem may have been the song beginning "The Zephyr that toys with thy curls"; if so, it was apparently mislaid, for it was not published until May 9, 1868, with a prefatory note by the editor, H. Rives Pollard: "Among the MSS. of the late Henry Timrod, entrusted to our care, we have come across the following graceful lyrick, which, to the best of our belief, is original." For typical examples of his album verse, see "But Once Mine Eyes," in Cardwell, p. 99, and "To Anna (Written in an Album)," p. 92.

27. Letter to Hayne, September 16, 1867. In quoting this letter and in printing the sonnet (pp. 59-60), Hayne omitted the sentence in which Timrod wrote that he had given the poem away. Hayne firmly believed that a poet should be paid for his work.

Chapter Five

1. Courtenay's letter to Henry Timrod Goodwin, November 21, 1898, is in the Goodwin Collection, South Caroliniana Library; he adds that the Hayne edition yielded $600, of which Mrs. Timrod "never recd one cent." According to his own manuscript, Courtenay's promise to Timrod to bring out a collected edition of the poems was made at the railway station in Branchville, S. C., in January, 1865 (*Memories of the Timrod Revival, 1898-1901,* Charleston Library Society). Emily's letter to Hayne, November 6, 1867, is in the South Caroliniana Library. Bruns also wanted to write Timrod's biography, but he retired gracefully when he heard that Hayne was to do it. In a letter to her daughter Edith, Nov. 23, 1867 (original in the possession of Mrs. George Munro Goodwin, Athens, Georgia),

Emily wrote, quoting Bruns about Hayne: "Go you and plant the laurel on his grave, while I stand by you with the willow. You were his oldest friend but I yield to no man the place I had in his heart." She added that "Bruns says that he is disappointed but yields to Hayne as the one best fitted to do the book, for that though he could bring no greater love to it, yet he was his superior in the art and genius that work required."

2. See Cardwell, pp. 14-19, for a detailed description of the proofsheets and for variant readings. There are enough inconsequential changes in punctuation in Timrod's best-known poem, the 1866 "Ode," to indicate that Hayne relied on a manuscript rather than on the first newspaper version; apparently he had not seen the revised version, as he does not mention it. He may simply have preferred the earlier version. In a letter to W. A. Courtenay (March 15, 1898; Charleston Library Society), Kate Timrod Lloyd wrote that "I lent Mr. Hayne these proofsheets and the volume published at that time was taken entire from them. They were corrected by Mr. Timrod." Hayne, of course, added later poems that were not on the proofsheets. Although Courtenay had the proofs bound and deposited the volume in the Charleston Library Society, the Memorial Edition followed the Hayne text. Cardwell, p. 14, and Hubbell, p. 33, note some of Hayne's dubious improvements in Timrod's letters.

3. I have noted before that in the *Memoir*, p. 23, and in the article in the *Southern Bivouac* (IV, p. 330), Hayne wrote that *Russell's Magazine* totalled four volumes, over two years. It is in six volumes and over a span of three years. Clearly Hayne had no file available. Emily Goodwin wrote Hayne numerous and voluminous letters; when the publisher suggested that, for reasons of policy, Timrod's war poems be omitted, she indignantly rejected the idea, because these were "among his best" (October 31, 1867). She wrote (December 21, 1867) that "I have in my scrapbook two poems published in Hal's youth . . . written for two anniversary dinners, an ode to Jackson the hero of N. O. and an ode on the battle of Lexington. If you wish I can easily copy them for you." Hayne did not use either poem. Cardwell, pp. 84-85, reprints the "Ode Composed for the Anniversary of the Battle of New Orleans"; it had appeared in the Charleston *Daily Courier*, January 9, 1856. Mrs. Timrod's feelings about the book were mixed. When Hayne requested some of her husband's editorials, she sent him (September 10, 1872) a few that were non-political. After the proofs appeared, although she wrote that "your biography is perfect," she remained justifiably afraid that if her name were linked with it she would lose her job in the Treasury Department: "Hal's book is very rebel, and they will use it against me if they find out I am the wife of the author." Hayne's letter to

Whittier, written before the book was published and describing the *Memoir* as "a very brief and simple one," is quoted in Hubbell, p. 115.

4. I have quoted from the second edition of *Florida* (1876), because it is apparently the one that Hayne saw; however, I have used the Centennial Edition, Vol. VI, edited by Philip Graham (General Editor, Charles R. Anderson), Baltimore, 1945, pp. 160-61. Graham quotes the relevant paragraph from the first edition of *Florida* 1875); there are several changes in the wording (e.g., at the end, "a genuine art" became "a dainty art"), but there is no change in tone or in meaning. Hayne's letter of July 25, 1877, is in the Charles D. Lanier Collection, Johns Hopkins University; it is printed by Graham, VI, pp. xix-xx. Graham notes that no reply by Lanier has been found. But Hayne's letter may have had some influence on Lanier. In the series of lectures given at Peabody Institute on *Shakespeare and His Forerunners* (Fall, 1878; published, 1902), Lanier included one on "The Sonnet-Makers from Surrey to Shakspere," and he almost drags in a tribute to Timrod. After reading Sir Philip Sidney's sonnet XLI on love, Lanier added: "as I have just read you a sonnet from one of the earliest of the sonnet-writers, let me now clinch and confirm this last position with a sonnet from one of the latest,—one who has but recently gone to that Land where, as he wished here, indeed life and love are the same, one who, I devoutly believe, if he had lived in Sir Philip's time might have been Sir Philip's worthy brother both in poetic sweetness and in honorable knighthood. I mean Henry Timrod." Lanier then read the sonnet beginning "Most men know love but as a part of life." I have again quoted from the Centennial Edition, Vol. III, pp. 94-95, edited by Kemp Malone. Earlier, Bruns had agreed with Hayne: even Timrod's brief works were carefully thought out as to content and theme, and distinctive for "the exquisite metrical harmony which he attained and which alone would entitle him to a high place among our native poets" (Lecture at Charleston, October 27, 1870).

5. Rivers' book was published in Charleston, without date and apparently without copyright, but probably in 1876; it also contains two long poems by Rivers. On December 10, 1867, Simms sent a copy of the lecture to Evert A. Duyckinck; this was the text published in the Charleston *Courier*, November 30, 1867 (*Letters*, V, pp. 97-98). H. T. Thompson, p. 54; on 54n., he quotes a letter from his father, Hugh S. Thompson, to John P. Thomas. On Nov. 23, 1867, Emily wrote her daughter Edith that, in Columbia, Rivers had addressed "a crowded and select audience Thursday at the college. . . . I did not go of course, but Katie did. She says it was beautiful."

6. G. A. Wauchope, *Writers of South Carolina*, 1910, p. 25. The

Simms and Bruns items have been discussed earlier. The Austin and McKinley poems were published in *A Timrod Souvenir,* printed in Aiken, S. C., 1901, by W. A. Courtenay, for private distribution. Simms also tried to be of practical help. In an unpublished letter to Emily Timrod Goodwin, Dec. 25, 1868, he wrote that a Baltimore magazine could get for Katie a $55.00 sewing machine "for $22.00 cash, and $33 taken out in advertising." The magazine offered to "give to Mrs. Timrod's benefit the $33 advertising." The machine was never purchased.

7. For textual details, see Cardwell, pp. 18-20. There is a remarkably complete file, mainly compiled by Courtenay, of the correspondence, in the Charleston Library Society. In a letter to Henry Timrod Goodwin, November 21, 1898, Courtenay makes it clear that Houghton Mifflin published the book only after all expenses had been guaranteed by the Timrod Memorial Association.

8. Ludwig Lewisohn, "Books We Have Made," Charleston *News and Courier,* July 5–September 20, 1903. Chap. XII is devoted to Timrod. In complete opposition to Lanier's point of view, Lewisohn emphasizes Timrod's rigorous work in training his poetic talent.

9. For these works, see the Selected Bibliography; practically all of them have been noted earlier. For the quotation from Hubbell, see *The South in American Literature,* p. 472.

10. William Dean Howells, in *Atlantic Monthly,* XXI (May, 1873), p. 622.

11. Letter to Rachel Lyons, December 10, 1861, *Alabama Review,* II (April, 1949), pp. 139-49. A year later, the poem "Christmas," with its insistent demand for physical and spiritual peace, was published.

Selected Bibliography

PRIMARY SOURCES

In this first section I have included books and articles that contain Timrod letters, since these have not been collected; the primary sources are arranged chronologically; secondary sources, alphabetically.

Henry Timrod: Poems. Boston: Ticknor and Fields, 1859. Has 1860 on title page, but the copyright date 1859, and was on sale before Christmas, 1859. This was Timrod's only book to be published during his life.

The Poems of Henry Timrod. Edited, with a Sketch of the Poet's Life, by Paul H. Hayne. New York: E. J. Hale and Son, 1873. Copyright 1872, but apparently not on sale until January, 1873. New Revised Edition, 1873; contains more poems, but no real revision. Hayne's text is dependable, and his *Memoir,* despite some inaccuracies, remains indispensable.

Katie. By Henry Timrod. New York: E. J. Hale and Son, 1884. An illustrated edition; text abstracted from Hayne edition.

Poems of Henry Timrod. Memorial Edition. Boston: Houghton, Mifflin and Co., 1899; Richmond: B. F. Johnson Publishing Company, 1901. The Introduction is by John Pendleton Kennedy Bryan; the arranging and the editing seem to have been done by W. A. Courtenay. The text is reliable, following Hayne when possible; but the poems are haphazardly arranged. No variants are given.

Verses from "Cotton Boll." By Henry Timrod. Richmond: B. F. Johnson, 1901. Embellished pamphlet; the "Official Souvenir of the Women's Department of the South Carolina Inter-State and West Indian Exposition" in Charleston.

The Uncollected Poems of Henry Timrod. Edited with an introduction by Guy A. Cardwell, Jr. Athens: The University of Georgia Press, 1942. Indispensable. Contains all the poems in Timrod's Autographic Relics, as well as other uncollected poems, with variants when any are known. Excellently edited, with a useful introduction.

The Essays of Henry Timrod. Edited with an Introduction by Edd Winfield Parks. Athens: The University of Georgia Press, 1942. Contains also Timrod's editorials which deal with literature.

HUBBELL, JAY B.: *The Last Years of Henry Timrod, 1864-1867.* Durham: Duke University Press, 1941. An intelligent but specialized study. Hubbell modestly lists himself as editor; the book contains Timrod's letters to Hayne and others, and many others to or about Timrod. Also very useful on William Henry Timrod.

MABBOTT, THOMAS O. (ed.). "Some Letters of Henry Timrod," *American Collector,* III (February, 1927), pp. 191-95.

FIDLER, WILLIAM (ed.). "Unpublished Letters of Henry Timrod," *Southern Literary Messenger,* II (October, November, December, 1940), pp. 527-35, 605-11, 645-51. Has an introductory sketch of Timrod's life. Letters to Rachel Lyons, "La Belle Juive."

————. "Seven Unpublished Letters of Henry Timrod," *Alabama Review,* II (April, 1949), pp. 139-49.

ROBILLARD, DOUGLAS J. "Two Timrod Letters," *North Carolina Historical Review,* XXXIX (Autumn, 1962), pp. 549-53. Written in 1865 to the poet R. H. Stoddard.

SECONDARY SOURCES

BRUNS, JOHN DICKSON. "A Lecture on Timrod," Charleston *Sunday News,* April 30, 1899. Delivered October 27, 1870. Often entitled the "Life and Genius of Henry Timrod." A perceptive, sympathetic essay.

CARDWELL, GUY A., JR. "The Date of Henry Timrod's Birth," *American Literature,* VII (May, 1935), pp. 207-8. Established the date as 1828, not 1829 or 1830.

————. "William Henry Timrod, the Charleston Volunteers, and the Defense of St. Augustine," *North Carolina Historical Review,* XVIII (January, 1941), pp. 27-37.

CLARE, VIRGINIA P. *Harp of the South.* Atlanta: Oglethorpe University Press, 1936. Pleasantly written, but inaccurate and uncritical.

FELDER, HERMAN M. *Notes on Timrod.* Unpublished M. A. thesis, Vanderbilt University, 1936. Much excellent material, ably presented; erroneous about Timrod's ancestry.

HAYNE, PAUL HAMILTON. "Ante-Bellum Charleston," *Southern Bivouac,* IV (November, 1885) pp. 327-36. A pleasant, nostalgic essay, useful on *Russell's Magazine.*

HUBBELL, JAY B. *The South in American Literature, 1607-1900.* Durham: Duke University Press, 1954. By far the best treatment of ante-bellum Southern literature.

————. "Literary Nationalism in the Old South," in *American Studies in Honor of William Kenneth Boyd.* Durham: Duke University Press, 1940, pp. 175-220. The best single treatment of this subject.

LEWISOHN, LUDWIG. "Books We Have Made," Charleston *News and Courier,* July 5-September 20, 1903. Chap. XII is devoted to Timrod. A perceptive and stimulating essay.

MCKEITHAN, DANIEL M. (ed.). *A Collection of Hayne Letters.* Austin: University of Texas Press, 1944. Useful material about Timrod.

PAGE, WALTER HINES. "Henry Timrod," *South-Atlantic,* I (March, 1878), pp. 359-67. Slight, but interesting.

PARKS, EDD W. *Ante-Bellum Southern Critics.* Athens: University of Georgia Press, 1962. Discusses at length the criticism of Timrod and his contemporaries, Simms, Grayson, and Hayne.

—————. *Southern Poets.* New York: American Book Company, 1936. Relates Timrod to his fellow poets and to his environment.

—————. "Timrod's College Days," *American Literature,* VIII (November, 1936), pp. 294-96.

—————. "Timrod's Concept of Dreams," *South Atlantic Quarterly,* XLVIII (October, 1949), pp. 584-88. Discusses Timrod's belief in a subconscious power.

RIVERS, WILLIAM J. *A Little Book: to Obtain Means for Placing a Memorial Stone upon the Grave of the Poet, Henry Timrod.* Charleston: for private distribution; no date, but probably 1876. Contains Rivers' lecture, "The Characteristics of Henry Timrod's Poetry, and his Rank as a Poet," delivered in late November, 1867.

RUBIN, LOUIS D., JR.: "Henry Timrod and the Dying of the Light," *Mississippi Quarterly,* XI (Summer, 1958), pp. 101-11. Stimulating analysis of Timrod's poem, "Charleston."

SHEPHERD, HENRY E., and A. S. SALLEY, JR. "Henry Timrod: Literary Estimate and Bibliography," *Southern History Association Publications,* III (October, 1899), pp. 274-80. Of little value. The bibliography is incomplete and at times inaccurate.

SIEGLER, MILLEDGE B. "Henry Timrod and Sophie Sosnowski," *Georgia Historical Quarterly,* XXXI (September, 1947), pp. 172-80. Definitive treatment of one of Timrod's love affairs.

TAYLOR, RUPERT. "Henry Timrod's Ancestress, Hannah Caesar," *American Literature,* IX (January, 1938), pp. 419-30. Disproves the ancient gossip that Timrod had Negro blood.

THOMPSON, HENRY T. *Henry Timrod: Laureate of the Confederacy.* Columbia: The State Company, 1928. By the son of Timrod's close friend, Hugh S. Thompson; contains some valuable material, but enough errors that it should be used cautiously.

Selected Bibliography

TRENT, WILLIAM P. *William Gilmore Simms*. Boston: Houghton, Mifflin and Company, 1892. Thesis-ridden, but indispensable since Trent used letters from Timrod to Simms that have since been lost.

VOIGT, G. P. "New Light on Timrod's 'Memorial Ode'," *American Literature*, IV (January, 1933), pp. 395-96. First established that Timrod's best-known poem was published in 1866, not 1867.

————. "Timrod's Essays and Literary Criticism," *American Literature*, VI (May, 1934), pp. 163-67. Competent but very brief.

————. "Timrod in the Light of Newly Revealed Letters," *South Atlantic Quarterly*, XXXVII (July, 1938), pp. 263-69. Intelligent but scant use of the material in the South Caroliniana Library.

WAUCHOPE, GEORGE A. *Henry Timrod: Man and Poet*. Columbia S. C.: The University Press, 1915. A good and interesting survey, regrettably brief.

Index

DATE DUE
